More than a Marathon, Touching the Edges – A Fine Balance

M.Y. Rite

More Than a Marathon, Touching the Edges – A Fine Balance

Olympia Publishers
London

www.olympiapublishers.com
OLYMPIA PAPERBACK EDITION

Copyright © M.Y. Rite 2023

The right of M.Y. Rite to be identified as author of
this work has been asserted in accordance with sections 77 and 78 of
the Copyright, Designs and Patents Act 1988.

All Rights Reserved

No reproduction, copy or transmission of this publication
may be made without written permission.
No paragraph of this publication may be reproduced,
copied or transmitted save with the written permission of the publisher,
or in accordance with the provisions
of the Copyright Act 1956 (as amended).

Any person who commits any unauthorised act in relation to
this publication may be liable to criminal
prosecution and civil claims for damage.

A CIP catalogue record for this title is
available from the British Library.

ISBN: 978-1-80439-281-2

This is a work of fiction.
Names, characters, places and incidents originate from the writer's
imagination. Any resemblance to actual persons, living or dead, is
purely coincidental.

First Published in 2023

Olympia Publishers
Tallis House
2 Tallis Street
London
EC4Y 0AB

Printed in Great Britain

This work is collected and shared with dedication and thanks to Ari.

Ari has been like an emotional guardian. He has caught me and sat with me holding stillness from busy-ness. This has enabled me to reach feelings from way down under. In this space he has asked me to pause allowing my invisible to become visible and my wordlessness to have words.

His belief and encouragement have given me confidence to publish. My hope is that this will help others on their journeys.

Had Ari not said PUBLISH, these would still be sat in the depth of my hard drive or stuffed in my sock drawer gathering dust hidden even from spiders, with hundreds of others and even getting closer to the shredder!

Some of the areas in this collection she shares about are:
- Old roads
- Leading to explore again
- Bodies break
- The motherless child
- Dad where are you?
- Loneliness
- Beauty and burden of silence
- When I am miles away
- The difference- the gift of therapy

Introduction

Maya was inspired by walking during the isolating times of Lockdown. She has gathered these writings some from now and some from back then.

This is Maya's first collection of published poems. For her they touch edges of a silent childhood and the perils of loneliness eased with horse talk.

Her silence and adolescence led her body to silently ask for help through starvation and of course reject any form of attempted connection except with horses. Maya went to university wondering about the purpose of life. She then leapt into a short-lived career. Maya found herself floundering as if a child ill equipped to live in an adult world.

Maya's work weaves its way through her sense of invisibility and many wordless years. Her work is often inspired by walking and being outside and wanting to belong. The externalisation of her words came about through finding a relationship with her body after years of misuse

Maya hopes that this part of her work shares some of her journey in a way to offer company to others on their own unique roads.

Reading this you may be walking alongside someone on their journey or you may be walking alone or in company, perhaps looking at a map to see where you are. Sadly, and gladly, there is no sat nav for any personal journey; their maybe emotional guardians on the way as friends, therapists and teachers of life.

Maya met many road blocks. Shortly after turning twenty-one, Maya spent eighteen months in a mental health hospital followed by eighteen more long terrifying months in a supposed addiction recovery setting. She fled into the world, finding her feet through riding horses, animal and child care jobs as a step back into a working world.

As Maya gained confidence she began to take hold of her life. She made career changes and started to find her feet. No road was straight. She talked at a conference about her eating disorder experiences. After this point she met her first therapist. They went through many emotional battles to find a precious connection. This was a new beginning and a very precious gift. As she gained confidence, she tried to meet peers through water sports.

At forty Maya living with her partner, was diagnosed with breast cancer. She began running and set her mind on the London Marathon. She took up cycling challenges too. She was on the go for hours upon hours searching for peace. If only that worked! Then overtraining while on chemotherapy led to wear on her bones and a broken clavicle and fractured vertebrae. She was prescribed walking and Pilates while waiting for bone infusions! London in 3 hours 23 was nothing in comparison to having to stop and to do Pilates!

Her body spoke **with** breathlessness, asthmatic wheezing and chronic gut **problems** as her vagal system froze. Never before had Maya been physically broken. Her body held many scores. Around fifty she experienced an onset of osteoarthritis accompanying her Osteopenia.

Eventually Maya realised she had met her limits. She was

then grateful to be allowed to build up to a ten-minute walk. She heard her body scream so loudly. It was when she stopped obsessive cycling, swimming and running and reached a point where she asked for help. It felt as if for the first time she could reach the feelings she had run from with a new therapist at her zoom side. It was from this place, that she collated her raw writing, edges of the past touched the here and now. At this place of stillness initially enforced by injury her poems became visible.

This collection is around feelings. Maya has 1000+ more and as she journeys deeper through therapy more writing emerges connecting to her once hidden body strata. In the future she may share more of her sock drawer collections. These have themes around longing to belong, her journey, on the run, outside in, the body of food, owning her body and further along her road who knows…

In this book Maya shares a small part of her journey aiming to help someone else find words and not feel alone.

In writing she uses both she and I; we, you and they. Depending on where the words took her.

Now Beginning to Make Sense

She had everything
She had parents and felt parentless
As if an emotional orphan

Living in a family estranged from feelings
She searched for an emotionally warm guardian
She felt so truncated
Alive and dead inside completely dead
And now as she reflects, she feels so sad
For all the years there was nowhere to attach
Nowhere to feel safe
As if she was living alone
Alone in a made-up world
She felt like an utter disappointment
Disappointment to them

She has lived frozen
Watching life from a glass vacuum
Seeing life as if it were unreal
And at times when a cell melted
She met life and rapidly refroze
For her then life was too much
She could not grieve the death of life
For she had not lived a life
She had not felt loved or love

At times she knew she was there
At times she was not there

She can see how she has lived in frozen silence
And it is now, as she gathers the threads of her life
And re-dusts the surface that she begins to understand more
Moments where music broke the deathly silence
She was filled with comfort, fear and relief
For dead became strangely alive
And then in silence the familial heartbeat of death once more

As she writes a first review of the frozen years
She is touched with sadness and disappointment
She understands how at times when you speak to her
She is both there and many times she is miles away in one scene or other
Until she has a task and work and then she is all there
And she is discovering a way to connect and make sense
Of how she flailed in the distance in her frozen times.

On Being FINE

The girl, she was fine (but not really)
She was happy (but not really)
She smiled to survive (but not really)
To the outside world she was happy, helpful, smiley
and they all said "She's so helpful"
That was not how she felt inside
Nobody knew,
Nobody noticed
She felt scared inside that was private
She hated because she was scared
The world terrified her
Nobody noticed her
She did not feel part of anything
She did not feel good enough
She did not want to do the things they did
It was all too busy, too loud
She kept herself away
Nobody knew how she felt, not even her!
She made food for them
She helped, she kept busy
Kind of doing nothing
And then she did not feel horrible
She started to stop eating
She aimed set her own goal
She kind of liked it, her own choice, or was it?

Then the voice in her head took over
She listened to it and ignored outside
It told her to obey and she'd have a friend for life
It lied
She spent years with the voice alone and scared
She felt glad nobody noticed
And mad and sad and nobody saw
For she smiled and she kept going,
She felt cold and alone
She found it hard to sleep
Even her skin gave up and crunched around her
She was good at weight reduction at last something was going right
Then it stopped, she felt scared and confused
So, she tried harder the voice helped her and scared her and it confused her
Nobody knew, she thought nobody cared
She heard nobody even if they spoke

She could not do the work at school or University
Her mind was drifting nowhere and elsewhere
She was scared of people and what she was meant to do
She did not know how to connect in everyday life
She heard them;
They said things, they called her names, they teased her
So, the voice was right
It was her and the voice that made it OK
She felt dizzy and so scared of falling over,
She felt alone
She told someone they did not see she had big buried feelings

they thought she wanted more attention
So, she told nobody, she was literally alone
Until one day it went wrong
She was in hospital where she was literally so alone
Covered in cold white bed hard sheets
This was beyond fear way beyond

Now as she looks back,
She wishes she had had the words
To say "Help me"
These are the words she would gift to anyone feeling so alone
The road was so tempting and not so pretty
She lost so many years building herself a life
Building trust and seeking love
She missed years of life because she had no words
She was afraid of letting down the world
She wanted someone to be proud of her
and the voice was

The voice was too big to deal with on her own
When she realised it was not about the food;
It was about the feelings that was terrifying
Feelings can be visited again at different times
In different depths and when she asked, she found.

At times she felt like a tangled fraud
For her journey to here
Is non textbook and yet she knows
Her journey helps her connect with empathy
She knows about her wordless world

She knows about
Getting up from hopelessness

She worries if they knew inside her
They'd see a fraud and take away
What she had made
They'd see her limitations
A woman in the rusting phase of her life
Trying to hide her oxidising cells
The metals of her mind

Forbidden

She, the little girl is desperately wanting a connection,
Any connection,
Seeking a forbidden land of milk and honey
Just hearing and understanding
Yet to her, the doors are slamming fastly,
Many she has shut by turning away and freezing
The harsh slam, like swiftly shut coffin
On its last sight to people
When one goes to this unspoken land
Timing unchosen by humankind
The land of silence and the forgotten
The land of no pain and of alone
The outcast land that was where she felt she belonged;
She stands on an unknown land alone of course
Seeing the forbidden land of milk and honey
The gates that once graciously bowed open
Warmly greeting her have changed
Expelling her as she expels herself
Spewing her beyond their iron spikes
Ironically, she's petrified,
And she pushes away the love she yearns for
Feeling barred as if there is no way in
She is locked out of death sitting here she feels excluded from life
She's sitting on the edge of life; his hand is held out

She autta be pleased, well, she is,
But is it within reach?
And still, she sees that forbidden land with passion
She holds her faded memories close inside
Yet to speak of the loss, the sadness is immense
For it was forbidden; banned
As the tempting apples in the garden of Eden
She believes she'd like to be with those who've gone
She'd at least like to understand
So, she can know it was not her fault they left
And move on with compassion
She starved herself of life
She felt to blame, hence she was living in death
Morose and morbidly alone
Caressing an unknown mystery
She felt excluded as she belonged nowhere
Not belonging hurts like hell
and is a comfort-
No one to let down
As if belonging feels trapped and voiceless
It seems that any world available to her
She slices herself from
And goes to her own undisturbed land of alone

The Story of Failed at Loneliness

She failed loneliness
It was safe to be alone and lonely
It was empty to be lonely
And empty to be empty
It felt too dangerous to attach
Too scary to detach
An island of aloneness
Was like a desert of the soul
Where the inability to connect was of insignificance
In trying to feel safe she was both here and not
Seeing her life slip away
With nothing to hold on to as a ghost of the present
Is present bound in a paradoxical powerlessness
Both frozen and boiling
Two vast extremes that define her fear
She thinks of losses
Conveniently sent to school a year early
A premature separation
The replaced dead cat
Her disappearing walkie talkie doll
No goodbye to the pony she adored
The family suicide was that her fault too?
Concussion from a fall, she told nobody
They went out as she slept in a different world
She was miles from their world

She could have died
In her world of Anorexia,
Again, she could have died
Nobody talked about familial death or illness or loss
She was alone and she failed loneliness
Her mother's cancer and nobody spoke
She was blamed
She failed at dying,
She failed at starving
She failed at cutting,
She failed at overdosing
She found her way through the dungeons of her heart
The deep red blood grabbing oxygen in her veins
Booming in her artery
All poisons as a venom of her life
And she survived and now she sits
Sits with a box of thoughts untangling slowly
Reflecting on the twists and turns

Teenage Life

Standing
Standing alone
Staring
Staring at the night sky
Standing
Staring at the night sky
Blackness
Wondering what is up there

They were all out at parties
They were out in town with boys
They all watched TV
They all had music

She was home feeling alone
Being alone she had silence
Alone with her companion
She was OK alone

The day is gone
Standing looking at the black world
The silence is loud
Nobody nowhere
The black universe
As it sits inside her all day

The cold death
Death in the woods
In the black of night
Was that her fault
Standing staring at the blackness
Staring alone and loneliness
Terrified and strong

Years later her therapist,
He said "It was not your fault"
Wow He was right
It was NOT HER FAULT
She felt a lightness in her step
A skip as she walked away
A Burden lifted
A freedom felt

Waiting

Waiting for the ring of loneliness to break
Like a child in the playground waiting for a real friend
A wish went wrong
For I'd wanted a friend for years
Forever wishing, hoping and waiting.
Then someone offers a hand of friendship
She said "I can help." This was too good to be true
Eventually I accepted the kind offer and went to her home
For a chat and not invited for tea like everyone does
That's normal right?
I didn't know
Someone reached out
She put her hand on my shoulder
It's late stay, stay here.
A lounge floor sleepover that's normal right?
Normal for kids and teens
Normal for young adults at university
I wanted and didn't want to go home as I would go via bins
For I was a bin addict
Phew, no squabbling tonight
No debate for discarded chips with the seagulls, rats and homeless men
And on the cushions in the lounge with a duvet
I fell asleep, the woman was watching me
I told myself to close my eyes and lie there perfectly still

This IS NORMAL
The door was shut, that was normal
Her kids in bed, that was normal
Why did she not go to bed?
The alarm bell rang was that not normal?
She sat in the chair and then there she was beside me
At the first break of darkness, I was expelled out the back door
I had to vanish and then go do a normal day
As if nothing had happened
The woman rescued me from bins phew
But the question I could not ask
Why did you watch me as I fell asleep?
Maybe a mother would a child, a nurse a patient
So, no voice no question, plain and simple bin relief
And blood freezing fear for night after night
I was clear from seafront bins
And then the next night I was led upstairs
"You will sleep better on the bed"
I never dreamt of the next
The wardrobe in front of the locked door
The curtains blew in the breeze
The street lamp gave me light
At least I was not beneath it in the bin
Now I remember the dismal dark house
I remember worrying about her children
I thought by being there I could help them
I could feed them and clothe them
I could buy them gifts and take them out
And then the woman, she touched me, she did not ask
Sending my head crazy with sparkling dancing inside

What was this?
She had found a zinging chamber of secrets
A feeling I did not know, wait, did I?
Yes, I did not know the feeling but not its name
It had happened cantering over the fields
What was it that was magical and sparkled,

And yet felt bad I was trapped without choice
It was better than the bins, or was it?
For months I tried to speak
I stopped my career
I sold my home as she instructed
It was from my grandmother's money
It was her son's suicide that triggered extreme family shame
In this emotional void I believed it was my fault
As was my anorexia which fed this shame
I had been looking for acceptance and belonging
The silence carried fractured shame,
Splintering hopes of connection
I was the girl, the useless one
I was worried about her children
About this secret life, nobody knew
Until one day, pushed too far
I left and of course I had no words
I slept at the yard looked after horses
The smell of safety
Smouldering wood shavings and sweet meadow hay
The quiet leaking caravan with melodic rain drips
I loved the rain
I felt the cold rain drops plop
I didn't care

I always wanted to work with horses
And then my savage bulimic beast rearose
It could not be contained single handed
In shame I went to hospital fuelling familial secrecy

Abstinence

Nil by mouth for fear to swallow
You swallow any rage
You will spit it out like a lama
There is nothing there
The world of nothing
How can it build silent rage?

My rage was silent
Then it bites sideways
A comment falls out of my lips
Too late, I try to swallow it
Who said that?
It sounded nasty
I hated what I heard
Is that the repercussions of unspoken rage?
Silenced and then it bursts out
It makes a crack in the armour
Like a wound with seeping blood
Then the serum forms a crust
An ugly crust
Another scar
Like sweat, this rage rips through my skin at times
And then goes silent
The skin regrows
It feels, it notices

It needs to change
Is it brave enough?
Does it have enough courage to say I feel angry?
Does it know what angry feels like?
And how it can be safe?
So, smiling, helping, doing robotically
Are strategies to survive
Survival rises higher and higher
At times my rage simmers and steams
Survival stands taller and taller
A battle of growth, a phototrophic growth
It bends to the light
Wherever the light comes from
It seeks solace

Whippy Cream

Like a tornado of whippy cream
Or deluge of builders' foam
Take the lid off
Press the plunger
Woosh
It, lavers up

Then when exposed
Evaporates
Disappears
Gone

Or extends
And clings on to every part
Or everything in its path
Takes the world with it
Was it real?
Was it fake?
Was it there?
Was it not?

So, fear of taking the lid off
Pressing the plunger
Will she lose control?
Whippy cream or builders

Expanding foam
That sticks for life
And crunches every time try to alter
It is held fast

Perfect

There's a simple fault with perfectionism
Striving for the unreachable
With its rigid plans and expectations
It's desire for systemic mechanisms
It expertly kills any spontaneity
So rather than struggle for perfectionism
She needed courage to let go
Let go of the rules that tied her in knots
Let go of the belly rumbling critics
She began to lecture herself
No one can take from you the person that you are
Why not seek acceptance of yourself
To trust the praise has no ties
If any comes your way
Use the criticism for organic growth
Growth of life not shame
Your perfect is solitude
Your perfect is your isolation
Your perfect is untenable
You will always fail
You need to move through your lonely
Yes, it maybe devastatingly painful
To let go of every moment of succinct control;
And be part of the team of life,
To learn to belong with a family

To learn to be part and not to push away
To connect not to snarl
Your team of one has been so empty,
Can you find courage to be and to allow?
And she screamed at herself
"HOW DO I DO THIS?
TELL ME HOW?"

And inside shuddered
A whisper roared
I feel as if I can never be good enough
I feel so unhappy and disconnected

Yoyo

She felt like a puppet on a string
She feels good if she can help you feel OK
Her emotions rapidly swing up and down
Her anger pains tangle inside
A knot of frustration evolves in tears
Unseen tears of despair
There is no regulation
She was afraid of meds to calm
Afraid to lose her vigilance
She noticed silence ruled her world
How she wished to feel in control
Yet how she was opinionless
Agreeing with her controlling mother
She cringes when she hears controlling voices
She remembers her mother always being right
The terror of any challenge
So, she cut off feelings
and became inept at silence
She learnt to obey
It seemed she did not care,
She showed no response
and deep, deep inside she was alone,
Starvation became her buddy
seeking a sense of safety and control
Her powerlessness led her to

a reliable relationship with food
When there was no one there at all
She knew not to ask, not to expect and she became self sufficient
She was a mini emotionless adult,
She turned down her emotions and many turned off
yet internally turned on high super high
She helped to be noticed, to be recognised and exist
She gave away anything and everything to be wanted
So, needing to make things happen
Seeking reliability is this the ground of her disorder
of her secret inner world and silent outer world mystification

Watching

As a tricyclic witness
Cloaked in silence
Hush shivers through her veins
Bullied into submission
Gripped by a frozen torso
She sees her soul float away
Lost in the abyss
The abyss of drugs
Designed to take away the numbness
From the tips of her toes
To the last digits of her fingers
To return her to a place of body feeling
But takes her brain
To a place she cannot find her mind
Her words went
They were in her head but would not form
The anxiety dropped
Yet inside she could not reach the anxiety
She could not reach the energy
Like her world was switched off
She was trapped below the water
unable to reach the air
With no language she watched

Some Roads Were Taken

To squalid places she went
Maybe to feel how it was
On the periphery
Maybe to externalise her inner mirror

She has negatives,
Not developed
Unframed
Stashed in the back of her mind

In a vacant moment
When her mind is blank
When the world feels gone
They come visible
Some play as cine films
The sound muffles
The tape blurs
She loses focus
As she did when her body was open to squatters
Squatters' rights?
No rights but she had left
They helped themselves
And left remains and ruins in her body
And so,
She built a castle

A fort
A mote
Where tears were locked inside

Walking Alone

Have you ever smelt a fire?
Or seen the bellowing smoke
Seen the scenes of destruction before you
And walked on in
Opened the door to join the heat
Knowing you would be burnt
And kept on walking
Knowing it would be exciting and risky
That you would be hurt
And kept on walking
Once you started walking
You had to carry on
To stop would be another fail
They would win

As if a warning sign, a red triangle
She feels the sign, she may not see it
She carries on
As if a warning sign, a red triangle
She sees the sign, she cannot move
She is stuck
As if a warning sign, a red triangle
She sees the sign ahead
She turns around and she hides

And there is that red triangle
She goes right in
As if no one thought she would
Their disbelief
She has proven she can survive
Go against any feeling do anything to fit in
There is excitement
And then fear
And then hurt
And fleeing

As with cancer
She could not tell anyone she had a lump
Her body, her breast all hidden cloaked in fear and shame
She left it for days for weeks she had no words
She knew it was cancer and she held her trained silence
For her body was bubble wrapped shame.

The return to self-exploration

Adult Years

Here we find her reflecting
Swinging thoughts
As if a crying toddler
As if a baby sliced from a womb
Plopped into the world
And left to cry under the tree
No one came she gave up
Waiting for warmth
Every drop of blood cold
Frozen in veins
White cold rigid
The day was busy
Dodging life in busyness
Seeking solace of silence
Then quiet fell
Voices, screams of laughter
Cackles of falsivity
Pierced the quiet bubble
With spikes of fear
In terror she stood
Swaddled in wire with barbs
Could she make it to nightfall?
Could she make it to bed without bowing to the toilet throne?
Could she make it to bed without drawing blood from her

cold veins?
Could she make it to bed without poisoning her cells?
The cells that were afraid of life, noise, music, people, movement,
And terrified of singing, dance and crowds
She was longing to be loved
She was frozen like an embryo trapped inside a tube
And unclaimed, disowned
Stuck where she did not belong
She was so alone
So lonely
And so empty
So, how had she made it through?

She Is Ok

She tells us how;
"My skin, was my gate keeper
I knew to be OK
I stayed hidden in layers
Like those of an onion
Layers that wrapped the core
The golden outer coat
A barrier to the tender flesh
As you penetrate the layers
With the blade
Some make you cry
Some too tough to slice
Some too a tender
So, as I say "I am OK."
My outer layer is secure- intact
My inner layers- have an heir of uncertainty
As I enter the day alone
I wrap a coat around myself
It pushes them away
And while the outside is protected
The inside moulds and rots
It's eaten inside
The inside eats outwards
I needed to unwrap my hidden layers
To understand my feelings
The ones I now feel
To be the best to me I can be."

Accordion

The accordion
It plays with no sound
The dance that has no moves
Miming the squeeze box of life
The disguised dresses of time
Swamped and squeezed
In famine and drought
Her dance partner;
Herself alone on the empty floor
Absent
Whichever dress
She is alone in a body
In a body that cannot move
Outwardly frozen from Inward desire
The body tangled in chords unspoken
No tears
No smiles
No make up
No jewellery
Femineity banished
Unidentified,
Disguised
The accordion strikes a chord
That no one saw
And no one heard

Nobody gathered to dance
The floor was empty
She fell

Fear

Afraid of out there
COVID 19 march is sneakier than mental health
You cannot see this coming
Which angle and where will covid strike
I am afraid
Years ago, I would not have cared
I would have wished it got me
Not someone else
Like with cancer I was not afraid
If it took my body, any part away;
Or my final breath
I did not care
Why am I so afraid of this?
Masked with fear
Gagged to silence
Sat there calmly breathing
Then an invisible gulp
No air comes in, no air goes out
Trapped inside
Bound and gulping for oxygen
The world is at risk
My stillness is momentary
And feels endless
Motionless and stagnated
Terror shifts like a random fireball

A tidal wave charges up and down
And flows with fear
I am in the grip of fear
A statue in speechless silence
I am afraid of out there
I will stay in
It suits me to stay in,
Isolation is comfortable
Not knowing is safe
Others are unpredictable
Another layer of anxiety
I am afraid of out there
Nowhere to run,
Nowhere to hide
I ran through chemo and radio
Running and cycling absented me,
From gazes
If I even felt fear
Now, this would be it

Frozen Anger

Anger burned inside
My fear charred and froze
Sit here, sit still,
As if in camouflage,
It hurts to move
My belly tide was raging
It ripped my gut
My insides echoed with loneliness
and hollow emptiness
Cold and vacant
I felt it like never before
The anger I ingested, it scalded
The fear shook as it subsided,
I was still alone
Empty and scared
That is how my anger froze
And charred my pores

Frozen anger: frozen hurt
Now, I feel anger
I feel hurts
I see anger:
I see hurts
I can now sit with hurts
I can now sit with anger

When the anger is heard
I know the hidden hurt is raw
Even though the hurt is gone
Hurt crawls in to the deepest cells
and grips on like a stalagmite
Woven into a stalactite
Gnawing inside like an invader of time
And now I can speak
I am finding words for the once wordless
So, the frozen anger can change form
My freezing as a transition from Life to Death
Thawing like moving from death to life
Gathering my frozen remnants
Seeking self-liberation

Passive Anger-PA PA-PA

Passive Anger
Rages beneath and Smiles on top
Like a swan paddling upstream in a crocodile infested river
Silenced by the call of duty
Obediently tows the line
It is driven to fit in
It continues doing with a compelling need for approval
For recognition just to be good enough
It seethes silently and smiles falsely
It does not know real
It fears real
Belly laughter is blocked
Rapidly run from
Friendship is threatening and dreamt of
Groups, noise, movement terrifying
It simmers in fear
The explosion would be ugly
Potential devastation
Destroying the world today
As the world back then
Shapes the feelings that bite below
As The Frost eats my toes
The thermostat is set way below freezing
The furnace burns inside way above boiling
Held in a controlled way that exchanges

Rage for energy and buries feelings from way back then
The sadness is too much
I feel false, like those pasted on Sunday smiles
That left with the last hymn
Wriggles rise as I approach inner sadness
Buried beneath the rage lies deep loneliness
Seemingly no reason or conscious hurt
Like Jenga, as blocks move will I stand
The silent forces built inner reflection
Silence was real and loud it invited me to leave places at scary times
Silence gave me peace to hear myself
And undisturbed time that too was scary
No one knew what it was like beneath the helpful surface
Where rapids ripped the shore,
With treacherous back eddies and the undercurrents
At times I dared not look beneath
So, a helpless expression of "Don't know" took over,
I took cover
And now feelings I can feel and talk about

Is Sadness More Dangerous Than Anger?

Anger felt dangerous as a child
Sadness never felt
Now she feels bathed in sadness
She is trapped
Her anger has nowhere to go
No way out
The anger is eating her up
If she does feel anger,
If she dares
She feels crazy, mad and insane
She feels scared
How big will it be
What will it do?
Her sadness is solum and serious
It keeps them away
There is no smile
There is no play
There is no music
Safe in sadness
And then it drops below the bar
As the disallowed rage gets bigger
An essence of anger like red rag to a bull
Soap in the mouth
Smack chase
The sadness holds tighter

It's safer to be sad
It only affects her
She can smile outside
And cry inside
How does she mask her anger?
The raging bull trapped in her rib cage
Burning ferociously
The destruction feels so powerful
It would rip out her guts and spew them on the floor
Violence to the insides,
Invisible to the outside
Sadness and no smile mask the inner intensity
She walks away
She stays alone
She waits for it to diffuse

Latticed

Latticed with shame
Encased in a belly of flab
Lost in a mountain of vitality
Desperate to accept herself
Struggling with the feelings
Feeling torn and shredded like a silent torture
She dared not touch the body she lived in
She despised it with complete silence
She took all she was given
The potent external blame
She ate whole
No questions asked
Accused
She ruminated on words she'd been told
Many years ago
She was blamed for a family cancer
She swallowed the blame whole
With learnt silence and zero resistance
Alone, compliantly believing it was true
She burrowed deeper in to her anorectic world
With destroying devastatingly lonely feelings
She felt she had something,
Something that in her control
Some power at last
Though it wasn't,
Not really

Blocked Protest

It was not safe
Even to object
Read the face
Watch every move
It was less predicatble than a knife edge
FEAR AND HUSH
Blocked any feeling

Systemic Pulverization

When the stress levels rise
When the pressure valves are topping out
Where is the emergency stop?
Everyone is on leave
Nobody is here
We need to pull together
The system storms on
Statistics, numbers seem to matter most
What about people?
The outside face marches on
The inside cogs are hurting
Everyone is stretched
Stretched beyond their elastic limit
Driven to survival
Where is the love?
Where is the compassion?
Where is the soulful meeting?
We need to build safety,
Our team bedrock,
To give us firm platform
A ground to stand on
From which we can work with integrity
Are we not mirroring mania?
The pain of outside of here?
The patterns of the systemic pain

We are harming
We are not helping
This was not working for her
With sadness she left
She said goodbye
It was time
Time to be kinder to herself

Destroyed: Nearly

Seeking an air raid shelter
As the woman vomited her pain and violations
All sirens flashing madly seeking voice
To pause her overt gratitude for being heard
And her overwhelming rawness before we had sat down
I felt under threat of annihilation
Her awfulness had so much power, and pain
I felt so deeply and the empathy burned her,
The woman terrified of connection found me wrong
She threatened me with her red-hot poker of blame
It was there to destroy my life
My apology fuelled the heat
I was speechlessly shaking with no oxygen
An awful place she blocked any repair
Then I felt the power of her destructed world
I saw her devastation
Far too prematurely before any pleasantries or safety
Every vulnerability exposed
Kicking myself my inner critic gorging on my error
The criticism internalised as if it drew blood
Until blood there was no more
Her words shredded me
They dug malignant craters through my skin
As I sat blamed and accused
Feeling destroyed, I held the woman's rage

Suffocating in her emotional pain
It seemed I was lost in dark dungeons
never in my wildest dreams did I picture myself here
My aim to help backfired
Somehow, I was trapped by her blame
Her words ruminated in my darkness
As my confidence and my belief shrivelled to nothingness
I felt empty, annihilated, destroyed
I felt the power of her devastation
The black silence eerily echoed to me that I was done
Done in
I saw the world I was building crash around me
I was sure I would be spat out
By pending complaints
I could not face my shame
I could not repair her journey
So, petrified of this experience
I reached out to travel my next journey
To grow a deeper understanding of me

Destination Detonation

All in hot air she complained ferociously
I went from best to worst in a nanosecond
Detonation ahead, High alert, Bomb threat
I sat on the razor-edged seat
Wondering when it would blow
When will she draw the blade?
How will she hang draw and quarter me?
I saw my life being slaughtered
I was now afraid of her potency
The threats came rolling in
Would I who witnessed the pain be asphyxiated?
How would she leave her mark?
What scar would I wear?
Just as she had been scarred,
The power is in her erecting her razor wire
Her impulsive rage protects her vulnerability
Her void in which sits her silence scream

For many months I sat upon a razor-edged seat
Watching every movement day and night
And not knowing where to look next
There were moments of recoil
Amidst soaring shame at these exponential potent levels
The view of not knowing feeling time as a ticking bomb
Should I hide and cower covered in treaculated icicles

Or walk with courage and pride
I felt haunted and hunted out and alone on a road
The road now silent gave more vigilance
My mind travelled spiralled round a mound of twisted thoughts

As I found courage
I digested that which I had ingested
And it reminded me of the changing scenes of childhood
Escaping in silence before demands were made
How I read the silence as trouble
Knowing the tornado could come at any moment from any angle
My own silence was always best in times of emotional fear,
My own survival kit,
My own uninterrupted space
I had always been dodging explosions
And often tidied their aftermath
At times absorbing the tail end of the quake,
And wonder how I had got caught
Within the field of bomb discharge
Which often stung for hours and days

Last One

I look at the horizon
I hope I will not have been
The last one who spoke with you yesterday
I hope you may have had some rest
And find the sun awakening to the new day
I know your pain is so deep
I know you hurt to the core
I know I have given all that I can give
And there is not enough to give
To fill this void
I understand how love feels rejected
No wonder I hurt so much
May I not have been
The last person you spoke to
And I look at the horizon
And I hold hope
Hope for you
And me

In Debt

The email triggers intrinsic paternal panic
Drumming in her head are the introjected words
Don't buy what you cannot afford
Don't accept or take give only
It should be black figures
She knows she paid
It's gone red,
She feels wrong, had she really done wrong?
She feels she has failed
She feels so bad,
She kept no record, no trace to track
She just sees red it aughtta be black
Minus money
She does not understand,
She stews amidst swirling confusion,
Her life mantra emerges
I AM useless… hopeless
Her panic escalates
She does not know how to put it right
Her paternal panic cuts her steaming cold
She doesn't know what to do
Inside is like a steaming spaghetti pile up
Knotted the panic and sadness get tangled
She feels mad so mad she cannot speak
She cannot ask for help

Her shame too high
She was mad she did not check
Mad she did not understand how
The bank had taken her money
Money once she used to give away
Give away to buy a friend,
Buying being wanted and liked

And so, her adult self,
Took her dates, her facts
Took her voice and made a legitimate complaint
She watched herself talk calmly
Through her web,
A mesh, woven by panicked feelings
She asked for help and she got help
She needed to learn to slow down
To check and to wait for this cost
Cost hours of panic and sleeplessness

She, The Forgotten Child

Forgotten
She is so timid
As a small child
She sees loud and feels wired
For she is scared to show her face
To let the tears pour
For she feels out of place
And needs more and more
And while being weaned
Wildly needing time and care
She never learnt unconditional love
She tells herself she must be brave
She must cope and prove she can
She can be big and brave and independent
And this just leaves right behind it
A youngering child
Terrified abandonment
Angry cos no one cares
Or protects her
For she cannot let them in
She feels a vicious squashing world
The whole world around her is;
TOO BIG
TOO FAST
TOO LOUD

She tried to hold it all together
She is exhausted of juggling every ball
Does anyone remember the forgotten child?
Whose wellness pushes her back in a preverbal hold
She is unheard
Swallowed deep into the forgotten world
Is it a wonder she resists words?
For she was the forgotten child

And to the Mountain She Turned for Love

Love that'd never found her
She looked up into the eyes of the sky
It reflected truth to her
She looked at the breasts of the mother mountain
And climbed into her arms
And latched on to her nipple to suckle connected love
She climbed upstream
Fighting with her tears
Which joined the waterfall
Harmoniously she climbed on
She knew she had to go up
She couldn't be washed downstream
Her mother's breast was calling her
For love and milk
The warm milk,
Calling with emotion she'd never had
She found power and strength
The child, she climbed in hope of finding
She screamed in agony
And was held, it wasn't fair
Why wasn't she given this freely
Tired, frazzled and weak
She reached the mountain nipple
And drank
Nuzzled into drink the wisdom of time

She was held and she wept with pain and joy
She screamed in rage
She danced in tantrumonioum
And slept,
She slept under the gentle sun
Suckling on the nipple
This was her feed
Her feed of life
This was her sleep
This was her mother
This was her mountain
This was her home
This was where her heart sang
This was where she hungered no more
Where her mind could rest

And so it was that she turned
Turned to the mountain for peace
She turned for love
For holding,
For understanding
Love that had never found her
She found stillness in the mountain

The Childless Mother And the Motherless Child

As a child she was an adult
As an adult she had no child
As an adult I am seeing my child
As a child she looked on at mothers she wished were hers
I wished as they talked to their child
I wished as they watched their daughter
She wished they listened to her stories- but she had none
Inside I felt sad for the absence
She felt stuck in an emotional desert
She learnt the rules of silence

As an adult she has no child
She wondered what was wrong with her?
She meets a mother and she meets a child
She helps them in the way she knows how
She feels the preciousness
And yet she was a motherless child
And is a childless mother
A childless woman
She will not be a mother
She cried I have no child to hold
No baby to rock and adore
No eye smile or mouth twinkle
For I am a motherless child
And a childless mother
I feel sad and empty
For she is a motherless child and a childless mother

The Burden and Beauty
Beyond the gate of envy
Sits a core resentment
seeing a mother tending to her child
those adoring eyes the warmth
Is that the feeling that rips through her?
Seeing the love, love she never felt
Then she feels mad
Then she feels inadequate
Hidden and forgotten
She feels rage and sad and alone
She resents the tenderness she sees
She aches with emptiness
She tries to accept
She triggers like a wild goose
Hissing
Her head bomb goes off
Shrapnel she tries to hide
It's out of control
It feels vial
And then she feels so sad
She watches a mother and child
And then she feels so sad
She has none
She feels empty
Boom vicious feeling escapes
She hears herself as a critic
She hears herself making a judgement

Deflecting the years, she has been teased
Repelling the times, she has felt watched
Observed and waiting for the criticism
She closes down
And feels hate, spite and disgusting
So ugly inside
For she was never loved like this
And appreciates the beauty she sees
As the mother and child walk bye
Walk bye as one
Hand in hand
Slowly and together
Such beauty
She cries

It Was that One Moment

I looked into a mum's eyes
her tears now falling gently
with her hand on her son's shoulder
and mine accepted on hers
when she felt that pain
the mum was scared
"I'm scared you won't come home
Scared no one will know who you are"

What are you scared of?
My hand on hers
She carried on
Holding her child so closely
"I'm scared you will die"
I hear how scared this mum is
goosebumps charge up my arm
the pain touches me

As the mum and child curl
Burrowing in to cushions
Buried in softness together
Their tears run
Mine felt deep inside

They edge to the wall

there is nowhere else to go
And there in the stillness they are as one

Together we met love and fear
Held in wordless pain
They are held

Is this one moment enough to hold?
to unite mother and child
as they leave
there is a new sparkle in her child's eye
and a cheeky grin see ya!

In this beauty she cried inside
The beauty of that connection
A bond she never felt
She had an if only wish

The Child in Her Mother's Arms

The child lay in her mother's arms
Where she could feel her mother's heart beat
And the child's child slept
At the place where feelings are met
Sadness and comfort connect

A place I see
As a mother sings to her child
Curled as if a baby
In her arms tucked up
A tear rolls down my cheek

In the presence of this beauty
I have no memory of this place
It feels a place I was never taken
The voice, the melody
Touches that lullabic place
And sadness comes

As those deep church organ chords
Would resonate in wordless silence
No tears were ever seen
Just as in a static congregation
The melancholy calls to me
As I smile
And sob inside
For the living loss

Diminished Gaze

You look, you stare,
Through your window into mine,
As if a picture in a gallery
I cannot bear being seen,
I need to hide
The more you stare
The more I retreat
The more you look
The more I feel trapped
I feel your critical eye
I know it is not yours
I paste my past onto you,
I'm sorry this intense gaze
Obliterates my compassion
I cannot find love for you
I see your bond
I did not have this way back then
I cannot digest it now
I shrivel away, I shrink
Realising my pain,
Stuffing in my rampaging rage
Triggered by your gaze
The pain slices me into slithers
Invisibly I glide away
My shame takes hold

I wouldn't block their bonded gaze:
Their love, so invaluable
And why was it not there for me?
I wanted to have this gaze
The precious gaze of a mother and child
The gaze that passed me by now penetrates with pain
It pierces my loneliness turning into poisonous envy
For the absence of a loving gaze and emotional connection
Punctures me
And in shame I push away what I want
So, dearly, so deeply
I reject the arm that is reaching to me
I block
I fear
And I long

You Were My Father

My father, my dad
You were lost for words
Emotionless you stumbled
There was no place to hide
You were just there empty
Where did this happen to you?
Because you gave that empty smile to me
I was afraid to ask, afraid to talk
Afraid to be seen
I wanted a dad, a father
I wanted to feel a home
I dared not disappoint you
For I could feel sadness in your smile
And I stopped smiling
Your sadness killed my hope
And so, I dreamt of being gone
I starved myself
You were frozen
I know you could not be there
I expected too much and I feel so sad
I see you and I cannot reach you
I freeze,
I hide
We may exchange a word,
Your anxiety may slur it

I know my words, my voice,
My feeling would break you
I hold passed down secrets from you
I feel disloyal
I silenced words to save your fragility
You are my father,
My father,
My dad
You had no words,
You have no words
I feel your pain
I freeze when I hear your panic
I expect nothing anymore
May I ask,
Where are you now?
Why do you live her shadows?
Dad where are you?

Buried in the Silence

You had no words
At his funeral you spoke
She saw you tangled in a pickle of panic
She heard words stumble and slur
Where are you?

She gets how silence felt safe
She knows you feel alone
As she sees you falsely smile
She knows you are hurting
She sees agony of a man
Who taught his girl she needed nothing;
To need was selfish and greedy
To owe was wrong

She is afraid we will not speak
It hurts you to feel and to speak
Others can hurt and be attended
Father and daughter hold knife edge silence
She holds a knowing and a sadness
She is sad she does not know you
And she holds a distance as a protection
And you will be gone with no words shared

She is afraid of losing what she never had

She feels it's too late,
Too late to find you
She feels father empty
She hurts and she knows
You would not want to see her tears
You do not cry
Tears would paralyse you
You would want smiles
You would cringe at her words and at sadness
She is silent and frozen and yearning love
As she cannot guarantee a smile
She stays away from your emotionally baron world
And she longs for you to hold her
She kept silent for years
In her will she would gift you the voice of emotions

Sadlence

Silence holds pain
And pain holds sadness
In sadlence we do not speak
The courage to break the strategy
To voice the pain
To say she feels sad
She feels hurting feelings
Where were you?
When I needed my dad
Where were you?
You were in your silent mask
Trussed in survival
Survivor of trauma
Wrapped in the wisdom
Wisdom of silence
Did you know your daughter needed you?
Did you know she starved for you?
She was hungry
She was starving for your love
For you to notice
For you to speak
To talk and just to hold her
You showed her silence
The honour of silence
She wants to give you a gift

To show you the courage of feelings
The role of words
How does silence feel
Feel when you are hurting
Feel when you are afraid
Feel when you are alone
And nobody came
The hours,
The days,
The nights
She was alone
She was lonely
She was empty
She felt unloved and unlikeable
Now she feels angry you kept silence
She needed active holding
She needed love
Where were you when she starved?
Was anyone ever there for you?

Bodies Break Dreams Shatter
Athletic Warning: Bodies Break

She didn't believe her body,
Her machine would break
But it did, she broke
She did not believe them, anyone
It was not her body that let her down
It is her who let her body down
She could not stop
She thought she was immune
She came inside
She bent down to untie her shoe
There she was stuck
She could not get up
She silently screamed in pain
The stabbing in her lungs
Stole her breath
She met pain as if for the first time
Crack, crack, crack 6 vertebrae went
Like a domino pile
Cancer weakened bone on top of
old eating distress
Body distressed
Carrying Battina from wounds gone bye
Every move she made
She saw her life disappear

Cycling miles
Running free
Pool trawling
Emotional survival
Grounding her feet on the turf beneath
Today she wobbled to the doctors
Fracture… thoracic…
Compression…wedge
The immense enormity of that spinal pain
A pain she has never known
Grabbed her and the shock
Stole her breath and stabbed her
She was floating
The sun it didn't touch her anymore
She had gone from whippet to sloth
She was so scared
Running was Completely off the specials board
She had to learn to listen to her body
She could hear its inner disintegration
She was physically broken
And her mind fired up It danced
She had an emotional journey ahead

When Her Body Fell Apart at Its Seams

When everything seemed so wrong
She remembers the day when nothing hurt
Nothing was felt
Nothing was seen
Now her body holds the degenerative score
A tear falls as she writes
An electric charge
as her foot touches the floor
She recoils to knife sharp pain
She feels it with tiger like vigilance
The roar of a lion protected her from her
She does not want to move
Her mountain of tears trapped inside
As her body is coming apart at it seams
She misses the full fabric
of her once mobile life
She missed too many days and years
Times
when she could have been in her body
And feeling enjoyment and happiness
Now, her body is getting old it is breaking
She can begin to get to know herself
Her stiller silent self
She hopes to find a way with stillness
Now she can walk again
May she walk with pride and beauty

The Old Survival Suit;

She cycled in the morning
when the world had not awoken
She cycled under moon,
under stars and the sun
She cycled down the hills
and around the bends
And thought of heaven
as the clouds danced on
She wondered how the angels lived up there
And who they gave their wings to
And how
Would she sink or swim?
Pedal on, pedal wherever she may be
However, she ached she pedalled and ran
She found her head emptied
She felt her heart beat,
She felt her breath as if for the very first time
As she flew along the roads
She found a moving peace
And as she climbed her mind stopped circling
She went to the hills when she felt so empty
She went to the hills to climb out of her low
She went when she felt alone
As she climbed, she felt alive
Brushed by the breeze,

And watched by the trees
She felt warmed by the sun,
She smiled at the branches that waved
and the flowers that wobbled she felt alive
Her shoulders dropped with calmness
The wind tugged your hair so gently
She found stillness in her movement
It moved her low
To a connection
A piece of peace

Another Hurdle

Awaiting the next operation
Worrying about feeling stuck still
With no wheels to pedal
She was scared
She cried
Worrying about being trapped
Felt like another hurdle
She knew it was not the operation she dreaded
It was forced to be still
Terror raced through her
A static recovery would drag
Drag her to unknown places
And a busy head
Would set off at 1000 mph
Who would help her catch it?
Like a circus of her mind
A secret head spin;
She had to act
For she was in fear
Fearing any dependence
The need for help
Fearing stillness
Stagnation
Stuck in the goldfish bowl
Seen

Being seen
With no out route
And nowhere to be

Broken And Stuck

As a shadow I watch you
You navigate beyond zones of your tolerance
And we are silent
Keeping peace as I know how
I am hurting inside;
I want to feel free
Free to just be,
Not to have to hide
Not to seek cover
Not to run or disappear

When the rain falls,
I am trapped
My body has so many pains
Like this I cannot be free
I cannot run anymore
I am afraid to cycle in the rain
I am afraid to fall and break again
Covid stopped the world I knew
It closed the gym and the pool

I built new pathways in isolation
I made a new platform
On which I could pause
I could understand

It wasn't speed that was hard
It was stillness
And I could sit outside,
Sit with friends
And notice my mind scattering
Notice the rooms inside
As I darted in and out of
Like a bluebottle
Buzzing annoyingly leaving a trail
A trail of potential disruption
Through the body battle
Osteoarthritis and osteopenia
And healing old spinal fractures
I learnt to begin to be.

Sad-joy

It is not with sadness that she weeps
But Joy, yes joy, she weeps with joy
For her body is alive, living and feeling

It was once a machine, a survival machine,
It laboured relentlessly with no food or drink
Running through long and gruelling days
It was there for a purpose - survival

Recently it broke
And ended in a garage
Mechanically unsound
In the body shop of life
No, it is not a car
It was a body worn out
Frazzled

She discovered its speed limit
As she lay immobile staring at the ceiling
She knew her life had to change
It needed care and an MOT
For it was not the mechanical metallic machine

She had thought her body was destructible
It was scary for her body to pack in
She was fighting for breath while holding back tears

Leaning out the window gasping alone
The voice she'd fought to find before was gone

She lay in silence with breathless lungs
Weak and weepy in a heap feeling,
She had feelings, memoires of past times in hospitals
Those she'd avoided for life, numbed on food
Then harming and worked
Her body now burnt out
Though its clouded fear was calling for nurture
Letting her think each laboured breath may be the last
Inside was crying for a mother like never before
She wanted to sleep, curl away and die
She needed permission to laugh, to play
So, as you see it is not with sadness that she weeps tears
For now, she knows her body is alive
And she has joined it to be alive
And so, it was she asked for help

Depletion

At times I have been depleted and unsafe
My world was low nurture and low challenge
I felt empty
Ironically, external low challenge is internally high
I need a focus to settle the internal thoughts
The low nurture gives longing
Longing I may never have felt before
As I pushed away intimacy,
As I kinda disowned my body
When I didn't want to be touched and longed to be held
Everything felt too far away
I felt trapped in a failing body
Because I actually heard my body say No
I knew I was broken way before I was done
I still had won running shoes left to wear
And I sat with feelings like a new revelation
Feelings I had not physically felt before
I noticed new limits and allowed closeness
I saw your eyes look at me
Your eyes saw mine and I melted
Your arms reached out to help and then to hold
I felt your strength and your support
I felt a warmth rise like never before
My prickles softened a little as I noticed and wanted
A two way want not a one way give all

I felt love that raced into me
Unexpectedly I knew I was still alive
And now at four a.m. as dawn breaks
The ruby amber sun awakens the summer sky
A time I would have run before and now
I can sit and reflect
I am glad I can walk in the sunshine and the rain
I can see you run; I can see you cycle
And I am glad you can
And I am glad I can walk in the sunshine and the rain
And now I can cycle gently again
I learnt a lot through this time
And the gift I found
Is being OK with me
I no longer have to run for hours
I can be OK to sit
To sit with you
And to be with me
I have found the best gift
I have found my life

Nothing

Nothing gives a buzz
Nothing excites anymore
Dreams they are gone
As if they got quashed
By an expectant rejection or criticism
Like pop that ran out of fizz
All the fizz fizzed out

She remembers the rush of sliding down the bannisters
Of sneaking a gallop round a closed field
She remembers the highs from starvation
Of her felt success in crumbing the kitchen portraying an eaten meal
She remembers the buzz of university where nobody saw her starve
However isolated and ill prepared for the noise
Starvation inside buzzed and covered the external torture
She remembered both fear and buzz of her swollen joints
And the buzz and idea of death
And then the gutted racing heart of being told she would be sent home
So, they did notice her skeletal fragile frame
Then in a timely fashion the bulimic bull took over
She sadly remembers the buzz of stealing bin food
The secret feast then the rush of the evacuation and the

throbbing sleep
She wonders how the adrenaline rushed in her time of overdoses
And how she felt alive and the buzz of slicing your skin with the later mending throb
She remembers wiggling in a tiny gap
Through a burglar proof tightly latched hospital kitchen window
To feast with terror in secret delight
She stole in shame and disgust
She had no voice

Then the delight of a real talkable high when time the boat soared across the lake
The waves breaking over the soaked decks
Saturated with spray and laughing
Real laughing, threat free
For the first remembered time with fear of an exciting kind

Then the fear buzz of being locked out while burglars were inside
The adrenaline that ran her up the hill and down through the woods
Puffing she was gripped white with fear
A rigidity held her as she saw her door wide open
Her home completely trashed
She remembers the frozen fear of living alone
 And then the buzz of moving in together
And holiday adventures

She remembers knowing she had cancer before it was

diagnosed
And since then, she has no body buzz as if every Buzz switched off
No dreams mean no disappointment
No requests mean no let downs
No cycling
No running
No buzzing about
She has to find a way to make her heart jump for joy
For it is as if nothing excites anymore

Sparkless

She simmers she smoulders
She swallows in silence
She feels left out
She leaves herself out
For fear of connection
She pushes away what she dearly wants
She pushes and rejects to stay unseen
And yet she wants time with you,
Just you
She is on her own
She goes into her own space
She pretends she doesn't care
She lets go with grace
On the surface and agonises underneath
She sees with love
The closeness you have
A thing she had never seen before
Like an alien landing on earth
Closeness that is real agreement and disagreement

She swallows in silence
She walks away flatly
She feels unloved
She wants you to herself
This is too much to ask

She did not sleep last night
Tossing with fret
She's done with what she needed to do
She's done her sparkles are faded
She switched off drastically in covid
She trundles by
She is OK when she is doing
She does not know how to love you
She switched out
She is elsewhere wanting to be here
Sparkles are out
She is not down
Just not glittery inside

Love And Toxic Love

Toxic love, a bite from a fly
A germinating sting
Unseen on the outside
It festers and breeds
Sucks on blood
Until the poison can be held no more
It erupts Puss oozing out
While an invisibility is sinking deeper inside
Whereby the toxicity meanders through the bloodstream
And freezes cells that did not know they were there
An inhalation of fear as a voice nears
An exhalation of toxicity paralyses any mobility
Then the inner toxic turmoil is broken
She feels elated and freedom as she finds voice
And guilt for the path of flight for what if it hurts another

And then she realises to love herself
She has to choose her nectar
As the bee worked
It gathered the nectar of life
It saw its shadow
The one it made
It wondered
Was it safe to stay?
Or

Time
Time to go

And so, she begins a journey
Her journey to love
To love herself
As she never did

Love is the place
Where night meets day
Were day meets night
Where there is no line
The dawn breaks and the sunsets
At the same moment

Where my tomorrow
meets your today
Where my today
meets your yesterday

Where these two meet,

Where they are held as one
One place one time

On Silence
Hush Shhhhh

Silence at the altar
Stillness they prey
Watching, looking, searching
In silence her mind can breathe;
Emerging from the depth of the gut
Oozing, rising
Treacherously, like an exploding mine field in a desert

Alone, barred
A sound unexpected
A noise expected
She freezes as her alarm sounds
Like blisters it pops her silence
Serum like a predator on her skin
The noise moves in
Until silence returns;
To over scab the wound
She is a dead picking
Watching every sound evolve

Silence strikes again,
The wings of her mind unfold
Like wings of a butterfly
Taking flight from their cocoon

On the back of the evening breeze
Spreading into the dark of the night

Her mind swells
She feels tears
Sadness
This is freefall
She does not know where it will go
If she finds busy
She can insulate from anything

Spinal Fluid

The emotional spinal cord
The fluid dances
To the music
Rhythms with the heartbeat
Drums through the silence
Through the taboo
The trap
The trap of goodness
Fills a well of emptiness
The deep dark depths of alone
She is in sadness
A toxic rush
Like a fear of the bottomless well
She watches the dance
She stands aside frozen
She watches laughter
She covers her ears
She hears movement
She turns away
The drum wades through
Through the frozen silence;
Beating out Taboo
Under the knife edge silence
Lies a place where words are suffocated
Silences stifled that say so much

and shhhed to nothing
hushed to the silence of death
Underestimated by many is the silence
as it had so many words;
all unheard
Feelings that are wrapped up
in hidden layers that sting
and make her eyes tear up with fear
Fear to let go
Wishing to find words
Fear to meet the outside world
The feeling that lies suffocated inside
Her world is overridden by outer silence
Keep schtum it will cause to trouble to speak
You will need to flea
For words can cut to a place of deep danger
This is how she learnt to endure silence

Talking, Talking, Talking;

Talking can be an armour behind which we can hide
Talking can be a way to push people aside
Talking can be deafening and make you feel unheard
Talking can be exhausting

For with talking does one pause?
One can lose oneself in words
One can be blinded from beauty
The beauty that lies in silence

One can talk one's way away from the truth
The truth of who they are
The truth from right inside
What a strength it takes to be silence
For just a moment of the day

What courage it takes to feel
To feel the feelings beyond the words
Deep inside your heart beat
The feelings that line every breath
Breath that your body breathes
To feel the hush of your being
To hear the heart beat throb
Lifting your gut
Beating out time

To hear how your sadness sounds
To feel how your madness rages
To play out with your childlike dreams
To move without correction
To be authentic to you

Take a moment
Quiet your body
Hear any neural alarm
Hear any piece of you that is unheard
Run in silent stillness
Run with the essence of you

There They Sit

Tears
They sit,
They line her eyes
Like silver lines in the clouds

There they sit
Tears
Then one
One tumbles from her eye
Like a first raindrop
Alone,
It fell from the sky

There they sit
Tears
They place her in space
They line her eyes
Like morning harr
A Scotch mist;
Hanging over a sea
Waiting for the sun to shine
The mist
You know the one
The one no one can see through
You cannot see in
You cannot see out
You have to wait.

There's a

There's a little girl who gets scared
Who sits deep inside,
When the grown-up patrols on
She worries she will be left behind
She worries it is all too much
She kicks and screams
And remembers feeling alone
She feels sad and mad
She does not know if she is hungry or thirsty
She does not know how her body feels
The grown up sometimes starves her
The grown up sometimes feeds her
The grown up does not know
How to recognise what she needs

They live together
Sometimes united
Sometimes separated

At the separate times
They feel many miles away
The little one drifts off
Waiting for someone to pick her up
She hangs on tight for the ride
And hopes someone will see her

And so, at times
She makes the grown up respond
And wonder where that growl came from
Or where the tears began
And they began way back then
When she was all alone
In a body that was an island
Surviving in Silence
The best way it could
Unknowing and unknown

Why Now?

What is going on?
Things were going well
And this is tough
Tougher than ever
So much sadness
As she stood at the gate
This lump rose
And two tears
Rolled silently down her face
Alone while the wind tugged gently at her hair
It blew her back into her body
Why does she I feel so sad?
She is scared of the depth of the pain
It was FEAR she felt FEAR

Vomit; Why now?

No, No, No
She knows what you are thinking…
It is not a gorge and vomit
It is not purposeful
She ate her tea
As normal now
Calm with no rise in tension
Then there is unrest
Aloneness and there it returns;
A frenemy from the past
No gorge
No high
No stealing
No finding
No adrenaline rush;
Just discomfort
A self-debrief
Why? Why now?
And she looks for the unrest
The trigger that fired the bullet
And she made sense and grew
Grew through
She saw the heart felt signals
And she knew she had to speak
To find a place to speak

And he was there
And she spoke
And now
She wants to be bathed in soft bubbles
She wants to be wrapped in rainbow coloured water
She keeps wanting to feel water running over her body
The water running down the contours of her skin
and then to lie in hot water
To be covered in warmth
Lump of disgust
It was there
This barbed ball
That once protected
Hard tough;
Impenetrable
Tangled inside fibres
Like the woven web of a spider
Blown in a hurricane
Trapping beneath a cold breathlessness
A stucken bubble
She could not hear her body
She could not feel her mood sinking
Waves of heat were rising
She had to remove it
Consciously she pacified
This bloated discomfort

Veins

Feelings run deeper than veins
Feelings that are thicker than blood
Feelings that have emerged
Over the journey of time
Bring a magic sparkle to the day
A sense of stars dancing in a difficult hour
A sense of complete closeness
When there are miles between her world and yours
A sense of being held
Held in the hand of your mind
Let's her feel connected
To the warmth of your tender hand
Running through mind
Touching her core in a way
That she knows she is alive
In a way that not even the sunrays can warm
We sail over the ripples of time
Her rib cage harbours safety
As she returns from her travels
She knows she has reached home
As her hand bumps over her ribs
And she can breathe once more
Holding her finger and thumb around her wrist
Something real and connected
She moves on into the day.

On Being Miles Away
The Driverless Bus

She is sat on a driverless bus
Ticket to nowhere
No one to hold her hand
She is sat on a thin ice
One molecule thick
The bus was empty
No one was there
She didn't even know
She is sat on a bus to nowhere
She has a ticket to no where
She has a ticket that doesn't work

Somewhere there is a bus-less driver
He is elsewhere
He has lost his bus

Like Playing Tennis

Ace
Volley
Smash
Volley
Smash
Four points
Love forty
And then you know
Then she goes where nobody knows
She cannot win
She cannot let them lose
and
Deuce, vantage, game, set and match
Well done she says not sure why
Because she knows that is what you do
Where did that game go?
Who knows?
She lost
She was elsewhere
Who knows?
Nobody…
In this space she cannot even gather parts of a jigsaw
She cannot find words in a search
She watched the sunset not the TV
Yet when she has a task;

It overrides her absence
She is on it
She is there
Every cell is there
She does not wander

Where Am I?

This is a tired place
She is jaded
Emotionally exhausted
Physically in deep sinking mud
Foggy air sticks around her torso
It is a rollercoaster
Trapped in a dream
Unreachable, she is unreachable
Small, she is small
Tiny, she is tiny
She is untouchable
Miniaturised in her mind's eye
Screaming to be touched
She floats away
She glides from earth
She's in somewhere
Somewhere is her home
Her safety is in somewhere
And as she whirls away
She leaves a vacant body on earth
An unprotected shell of existence
She does not understand
Her world never stands still
Something stops her landing in herself
She is on the run

From what?
Why is she not safe to land?
Why is she scared?
Scared of ending?
Dying? Losing? Leaving?
Or scared of connecting and loving
Scared of failing
Being engulfed in her absence
Lost,
She is lost and muted
This makes her voice dizzy
Senseless confused
And to survive she stares
She makes her stare an absent stare
That stare is her being present
For she is empty
For she is void
She must stay separate
So, she is here,
She feels so small

She Hates Me

She hates me being spacey
And she doesn't understand
Understand why
What she needs to know is I do it
Cos I can't bear being me

I'm scared I'll be eaten up by someone
I'm scared I'll contaminate someone
Basically, if I don't speak
If I don't let me speak
If I don't let me out
I won't feel the hate
Will I get out unscathed

Limiting words I hear
Limiting words I speak
For words interrupt me
And I worry I will forget
The words I need to remember
The words I need to say
I stutter Don't know
Like a safe blanket
When will it ever be OK?

You know I know something's not OK

That I don't have word
I feel lost in a vat
Unsure of where it is going
And where to go

Where Are You?

My partner often finds me in another room,
Awaiting a reply not knowing where I am
My body is there and I am gone
At home, on my bike and walking
I am in another room
He is right, often, I am not there
I am in many internal rooms all at once
I have to find a response
Fully glazed
I may not know where I am
Or what he is saying
Or what he or you want
I may simply have no idea
and an idea I need to speak
Senseless random words come out
We are missing out
I feel sad my mind fragments
My thoughts shatter and scatter
I hold on to the fragments
There are too many and so
I am darting between many scenes in my life
You know,
I failed English several times
Yet I live simultaneously
Writing my world

Directing a scene
Producing another scene
Watching behind a curtain
Not even invited to act
Or be in the audience
I peek a view
Imagine a role
And on to the next and back again
No time for an ice cream at half time!

Thank you for noticing my glaze over
It has helped me look
I hope to understand me
And connect our time

When This Began

I had no audible words
I was low,
I was flat
I was empty

My system was depleted
I needed you to hold me
I needed quiet space with you
I felt alone inside

I shut my eyes to shut out the world
I shut out the sunshine, the bird song
I was in stillness I was in silence
And then my inside world begun
I drift from here to there

As I opened my eyes
Behind a glazed screen
Like being a spectator to a stage
I was not in your world
It is as if I was an audience of one
Yet I did not know what I was watching

For I was in my world
It is safe and miles away from you

I was lonelily alone,
I was low,
I was empty
I was flat

Real-Pretend – Survive

She lived pretend
She acted real in pretend
She was pretend
She saw outside with fear
And yet she longed for outside
She stayed inside and pretend
For her pretend is real
She stays pretend to survive
She knew to protest was a pricey risk
She knew to dare to feel was too expensive
For she'd risk losing her real pretend world
So, tell me are you real?
Am I both pretend and real?
And are you pretend or real?
What is real?
For she lived in pretend to stay alive
Her real is pretend
Every breath is pretend and real
So, pretend is real…
And who is real?
She saw the "real" world with my "real" Eyes
She was not in it,
For safety you understand
The real world was too dynamic
Too busy, too loud, too everything except silent

It had its own sound,
The sounds of silences
She heard each silence and read them
Did you ever hear what she heard?
She could not interact
And as she went back to her real home
She had to pretend
She could not be real,
She could not protest
For a protest of any kind – was severely banned
Her mouth was cleaned with soap and water
No wonder she washed her bulimia out
To rid her shame, the filth, now that was real
The rest was pretend
As in pretend it did not matter
She could not reveal her real
She was scared of your real
So, her real was a convent of existence

Snow White's Coffin

Living in her glass screen meant none of you knew
For she was both there and not there
In fact; she was never there
It was so bone bitingly cold
She was not there
She would not have got here
For your real she did not see
She saw her real, her world
You did not
She saw your world but was not there
Her world was the only thing she had
Nobody would enter
Not even any of the seven dwarfs
For they did not know she was there
Now he asks her to find words
She has so much to say and nothing

About the convent of childhood
In childhood she took an oath of silence
Look if you dare
Do not ask or want
Give away what you want
Do not receive, give only
Pretend you do not care
Pretend it is fine and it is

Never ask it is greedy and selfish
Smile to the real world
They will see you are fine,
You do not have feelings just smile
Keep helping and you know you are fine
You will respect and do as you are told in silence
If you obey the rules of the real world
You will hide inside and
This way it does not touch me
For I am encased in pretend
Pretend is real and real is pretend

Self-talk

You say she lies
She's hiding
Hiding the truth invisible-ising her shame
You say she is angry
She knows that's what you see
Are you afraid of her?
She wants you to know
She is afraid, she is so scared
She is just protecting you
She is protecting herself from her fragility
From her very own vulnerability
Her vulnerability was abandoned

You see the bigger the outside
The faster the world, the bigger her feeling
The bigger her need
So, what you see is an x-ray to her soul
An MRI of her inner core, the lie you see
Is an invitation to connect with her hurt
Her pride is too tall, too tall to tell you
so, she buries it in rage

She buries her tales, building them taller and taller
She wants you to catch her, catch her hurts
She wants you to get her, get all of her

She knows you hurt too?
She feels she is failing you?
She feels are you ashamed of her?
She questions and questions, is she wanted?
She questions and questions is she loved?
She wonders if you will help her and stay with her
She knows she is lonely
She feels she is wrong

She wants to be close and paradoxically wants to be free
She wants to be close enough to feel
To feel is she is real and if you can feel her
She worries you will not like her or will take over
So, she lies, she hides so you cannot find her
Will you wait for her?

She wants to be seen and she can't tolerate being seen.
She needs your love and she silently pushes it away,
How confusing the conflicting messages,
The momentary contradicting signs
Get away and don't leave me

Listen to Me

When I needed to be loved
No one was there, no one heard, the call was silent
When I needed love, the unconditional kind
No one was there, no one heard, the call was silent
When I needed some love
No one heard
Was I sad?
Was I empty?
I don't know
I was alone
So alone
I must have felt so sad
I must have felt so empty
So alone and sad
And nobody saw because I smiled
That vacant learnt smile
The one I saw on Sundays
Layers of smiles and lines of pews
My eyes were empty and far away
Maybe I hoped this would hide me
Disguise me
And wondered if someone would know
And they didn't
They carried on talking
And I was not there

Girl within the Envelope

She cannot reach the window to see out
Until it is shaken

Then she gets a glimpse
A view
When she gets a view; she dodges

The envelope crunches in a hand
She hears the world whizz round outside
She cowers hoping not to be seen

Then the envelope is held up
Held up to the light
There she can be seen from the outside
And still cannot see out or climb out

Inside she is sealed in
She is silent in familiar
She is there and not there
Her true voice is she afraid of it?
She wants to get out
And fears what the world needs her
What shape she will come out
So, she stays in and torn apart
And gums her up

She goes where she is put

So, she climbs to the fold
She wonders what it will look like;
She finds the stationary
She writes her own letter
She wonders how to post it to her world
To believe from the vault in what she writes
To have the strength to be seen
To stand alone with her truth,
To hold her basket of gathered pieces
To find a route of stillness with her emotional circle
To make sense of her unconnected

Girl in a Bubble

What are you doing in there?
Why do you stay?
Does anyone know you are there?
Do you want them too?

Can anybody see her?
Can anybody see me she cried?
She cried alone
She's pushed away everything it seems
To keep her world at one
She's made a me on an outside
Unable to go in
Unable to get out
Watching in the sunshine
Watching in the rain
Floating
Her disconnection worked
To extreme nil needing
Her bubble insulated her
From feeling the world,
The one you are in
Maybe the world she did not trust then
And now she needs a bridge
Now stuck
Outside looking in

Inside looking out
People are not real
Well, some are
She is in her bubble in the shadow
The shadow she made
She walks inside and cries
Not many know how sad it is
And how mad she feels
Trapped in emotional coldness
In a body that chilled as a child
Feared a smile and feared warmth
And longed so much

So, she sees her part
Say no
Say nothing accept nothing
Make no comment
Stay silent
Even if you have words
Do not trust
Your words will change
Do not speak
Have no accountability
As you reject and push away
You see them walk away
You seem rude
You are not
You seem disconnected
You are
You seem that nothing matters
You are switched off

You are floating in a bubble
It can be free
It can be a prison
In can be like bubble wrap delivering a person
People turn away they don't bother you
People turn away that wont bother you
They leave you in your bubble
Floating
And you pushed away what could have been OK
Why are you so afraid?

You are afraid to connect
Afraid to disappoint
Afraid of warmth and it being real

You can do a hi-bye as you walk past admiring a view
No investment nothing lost
Meeting a countryside smile
When it may mean more unless it really is connected
Connection, it is unsafe, so you go off

Through the window, he sees her
He waits
She is frustrating at times
She just puts herself down
She locks herself away
And where is the congruence to a confident empathic worker?

She fears if her bubble connects it will burst
And the rainbow will splat

More on Loneliness

Pebble in white,
You feel on your own
You feel empty
You feel odd
You feel alone again
You feel awkwardly placed on a beach
You feel you have to give to be accepted
You feel to take or ask is wrong
I hear this and I feel sad
For you are a pebble on a beach
You are you
You are there because you are you
You are in the sculpture on this beach
I am glad to see you

Her Silence

Did you know silence had many depths and tones?
Do you hear her silence?
It's beauty and burden
Yes, you do hear her silence.
You know it has words
Many words as yet unspoken
From beauty and stillness of a girl
A girl with her hair flowing in the breeze
as her pony walks through the sea at sunset
In beautiful silence you hear her stillness smile

To a devastating inner thrashing of an eel trapped in a net
The burdenous toxic silence of inadequacy
As her heart beat thrashes against the rib cage
Like a tide trapped against the stream in a tidal gate

A worthless silence heard in the hush of the church
Where the organ bellows introject the psalms of shame
With a tone of morose melancholy of disbelief and truth
They shuffled forward and there she sat the sacrificial lamb
With this crowd are smiling telling her she was not worthy
The loneliness too hideous to have words
A breeding ground of poison with the intake of invisible toxicity
To a dismissal of existence with no worth to speak

To close her eyes in this stabbing silence was too dangerous
For they cannot be seen and she is attacked by words they speak

Like the silence of rape
A poignant pain that was a black hole
Opens holding a hidden loss
She is hidden in loss, she is hiding
Hiding in loss
She drove herself deeper and deeper
Into her mind which had no limits
It could go anywhere
Death was her companion, her comfort and confidant
For there; connection was her wish for normality
And where death a model of penultimate disappearance
An unspoken ending
Acted as the temptress of freedom
and therein that silence she kind of finds heartmony and peace

To a rage where a heartbeat crashes ferociously at her ribs
She hushes it so skilfully
Breathing disallowed envy and the if only's that never came
She was alone
And now she may find a beauty in silence a stillness
To see her world unfold with voice and connection

There Is a Child Standing There

There is a child standing there
She's standing on her own
All alone, crying all alone
Crying on her own
No one is there, not a soul
There are people standing all around
Scaring that child for no one is there
Cos there is no one really there
They are there and not there
There are strangers some she knows
And still, they are strangers trying to help
Help that child breathe
They see her, they see her pains and her tears
Yes, somehow that pain cannot be held
No one can hold that child
There is a child
Who's feeling so small
Small and insecure
She feels that she has lost her strength
Lost her fight, lost her will
Lost her dream
She has lost
She feels she is sinking into a ground cloud
And as with every journey no road is straight
She is not ready

There are ups, big ups
And downs, huge downs
And of course; big bends
And as, as with any cloud
The sun can go, yet it's not gone, it is there
This is her strength, both gone and there
Gone and there
If she could trust other people,
They would help her,
Protect her, even love her
And she is scared to let them close
Her eyes are on alert
She needs courage to let them in
To regain her strength
To re-find her- her;
To dream again
To live her hopes and dreams
To rekindle her dreams
I know she will.

Have I Ever Told You;

I long to be held
Touch me

There is a divide in the road
There is a rule unwritten
Written through pain
On the endless potholed tarmac
We do not cross the white line

Yet I feel alone
And I fear the cost
While yearning comfort
Did you ever just hold me like,
like a child holding a precious bear?
Why or why not?

What changed?
My cancer?
My broken bones?
As I turned away from your breath
My disdain of lingering stale tobacco
I turned away
And wished for more
Well, did I
Yes and No;

For the inner pain
Was masked in silence
You did not know
The paradoxical piercing pain I felt
And the bind of connection I longed for

Hold Me –She Wants to be Held

She stands so strong
She gives so well
But I am so small
I want to be held by a mum
I want to be held and not possessed
I wanted to be loved and accepted as me
I want to be looked after and to feel special to someone
She charges on
She seems so strong
She leaves me behind

I cannot cope
I'll corrupt her
If she goes on
I will say No
I'm drawing her in
Into my darkness
She has to understand
I was left there
She must come for me
I'm so anxious of being left
I've not been naughty
She just doesn't understand me
She, that bloody adult
She doesn't hear me

So, all I can do is flee around
And leave her
Leave her there
She won't fight here and now
She stores it up and up and up
Then I'll be so fucking confused
I'll explode
She's so afraid to be angry in present
With people she needs to help her
But she doesn't hear me
She doesn't help me
She leaves me behind alone

Unwarranted

The rape
Not justified
Not asked for
Uncalled for
Yet there was no, NO!
No objection
The voice of silence
They took all the wanted
And left the remains with an absent gaze
And a pasted smile
Loaded with fear
That sat back stage
The ricksha of tension with unconscious revolution,
Nothing sat still
Nothing felt at ease
It had to be emptied
In a violent self-violation
A tremor of anticipation
Sadness and anger entwined
Maybe that is why
She will not shut her eyes
Not now, not when you are there
No, she won't shut her eyes
For she cannot see where you are
Or read your face

Or know your move
She will not shut her eyes
Not yet.
At night
Years ago they broke in
She was away looking after another,
She came home
She could not get in
She hiked into her garden
Invasion alert
As if confetti her underwear strewn across the terraces
The neighbour offered support
He went too far
Violated
Raped
She was so scared of being home
Home alone
She was trapped
She was alone
She wanted a friend
Her shame gave her no voice
She could not object
Invaded with objects stuffed inside
She was lost in a sea of fear
And so it went on until no more

And she changed the locks
And still her home was burgled
Her body too

Decision Making Dilemmas;

Red-blue-red-blue-red-blue
Whichever royal head
First? Second? First? Second?
Which stamp?
Fast or slow?
Does it really matter anyway?
Which way is the pain quickest?
And the anxiety least
She contemplates choosing
Wrong one?
Right one?
Who knows?
Before the envelope touches the bed of mail
Inside a curious red box
Before it is even lying waiting
Her reply is scratching with a quill
On shiny paper reflecting the incomprehensible feeling
Nothing is held
Etching inaudible concepts into her skull
Illegible words form a knot of anxiety
That toss around
Why did she write it?
Let alone send it
Her brain was on fire
The etching was deep

Why would she talk about it?
Why would she talk about anything?
Because the silence is persecutory and loud
And there are words that have no sound
Silence of speak
Right or wrong
How will she choose?

Awkwardly

Quietly, Silently
She stands in the corner
The corner of a crowded room of 3
Look for a chair,
Look for job
Look for the door
Look for a child
She's scanning continuously
Searching for smells sights
Listening for moves and sounds
Her body holds the memorised smile
Instantly she slips away
The gaze stays
The gaze cannot hold a conversation
It is alone so silently
So sleekly she abandons her body
Awkwardly

There's a girl in the shadows in a darkened room
She's sheltered there hiding
She doesn't want praise
She doesn't want thanks
She does for you as she's trying to connect
She doesn't want praise and she doesn't want thanks
And she does and she shadows

Underneath the successfully completed assumptions
Resentment antagonising curdles her guts
As a babbling brook
A continual noise
A continual drive
If you notice her, she hides, she rejects
For she knows nothing is good enough
She cannot be loved for she is not perfect
There's a girl in the shadows in her darkened room
She doesn't know how to come out
She is sheltering
Nobody else knows
She is stuck in a senseless world
That looks safe outside

Oblivion

Do not take me to a place of stillness
Where you want me to close my eyes
And go places that make trance
These are not safe
My world grows into something else
It gets scary
My world engulfs me
Do not take me to a trance,
My unconscious overrides
I am scared and cannot move
It has power, so much power

For I am not there
There I am not there
For I am not here
Here I am not here
Emotionally I have gone
Do you care enough to find me and bring me home?

Bring me out of that sordid room
Shadows in the dark were my friend
As I watched the shadows dance
As I saw people move in the patterns
Of the carpet and the curtains alike
I was there and I was not there

I remember, it was there that it began
Barricaded in night after night
A silency locked in upstairs,
Body and soul both afraid and still
Dreaming to be freed
Wondering what normal is
My body was trapped
My mind had no way out
Was this belonging?
Yes, and not really

Close Your Eyes

Gently so gently they say
They invite so invitingly
Her flag of vigilance is ferociously flying red
Do they not know what happens?
Do they not know how frantic the brain becomes?
They say so sweetly close your eyes
Like an overdose of candyfloss
No, for in closing her eyes the world goes crazy
Pictures from out of no where
Scenes and words come alive
She is alone and scared
Does this happen to everyone?
Or is it just her
The random brain synapses cause so much turmoil
And she knows when she closes her eyes
They are staring at her
She has lost her front window
Loudness takes over
It is very loud
And smells where are you?
What are you doing?
No, she will not shut her eyes
Not just yet
Not on a course with work
Or a self-chosen course

She is afraid not of not seeing
More of the awakened world
It is not a gift to her
She does not understand what others soak up
In meditation, what is it?
Where do they go?
She sits left alone in fear and anticipation
Her heart pounds and sickness creeps over her
It is not for her
Not just yet.

When You Close Your Eyes

You close the door
You leave her
Your draw a blind
A cold thermal curtain
A moment of cold
It maybe for a moment
She feels you go
She feels alone
She feels abandoned in emptiness
Sadness and anger
You are leaving her too
In this place that has become sanctuary
A secret sanctuary to the outside world
The home to the hidden inner being
And now, at that moment feels unhomely
Echoey empty

Her shame stands tall
It now protrudes bolt upright
Does she tire you or bore you?
Why do you go?
Where do you go?
You retreat
Is this too helpless?
Is this too much?

Is she too much?
Is this hopeless
You are fed up with her...
She is feeling raw
Hidden in the smile
The disabled disabling smile
The smile that paralyses feeling
Trapped like a mosquito in a net
And being on her cycle recycling
Round and round

Are we getting nowhere?
Is she wasting your time?
When you close your eyes
She does not smell where you go
She does not taste the presence
She feels the absence acutely
Fear grips her insides
Will you come back?
What will you think?
When you close your eyes to think
The curtains close the connection goes
She is sat in an auditorium alone
No scenes the curtains are drawn
No ice cream interval
The doors are shut
Out of time

Left
Like the little girl alone
All at sea with no words

She will always feel alone
She will always be alone
The record got broken
It plays on crackling over and over jumping lines
These are the only two lines engrained
In the record of time

When you close your eyes
You leave her
It maybe for a moment
She feels you go
She feels abandoned in emptiness
Sadness and anger
You are leaving her too
Like they all do
Because she pushes them away
In this place that became home
And feels unhomeley
Does she tire you or bore you?
Why do you go
Where do you go
As you retreat, she is alone
And conversely, paradoxically
She does it too
She can have her eyes open and be gone
She can have her eyes closed as if asleep
When she is wordless and over-whelmed she slides away
She cannot tell you where she goes or why
She leaves you where you are
And you get so disheartened
For she is gone when you wanted her
She is sorry, she absents without a word

Expensive Was

The cost of loneliness
Expensive
It had no bounds
It entered every cell
The cost was priceless and unpriced
It was hand made
And lasted forever
Priceless, endless, engulfing loneliness
Whereby she found a way it did not matter
She found a way to not notice
She thought about something and held that thought
Carried it into a narrative with no reality
Until the new thought train arrived
And on to that she jumped
No matter where it was going
No matter where it went
She would be a loyal passenger
And her raw vulnerability followed any cult
As if a servant to that rule
A Cinderella who'd do anything
ANYTHING
Who'd befriend anyone because she was so lonely
That way she was never alone and really alone

The Sky Was Her Friend

She was not alone
She'd look up in to the black night sky
To the odd star
To the constellations of stars
Who put them there?
Could she go too?
Abandoned
Maybe they'd hold her
And love her

How?
As she dreamed into the sky
The vast world of the sky
The freedom
There was no alone
Where her mind wandered limitlessly
With no limits
When her mind wandered
It found a kinda peace
And then when she came back
She was in her bed
The stiff cold cotton sheets wrapped her in emptiness
She opened the curtains and stared at the stars
She watched figures form in the clouds
Watched the sky change to pink

The birds awakening the stage of the day
The animals on the farm screaming
The lorry stalled;
The men shout out as fresh straw was shaken
See, she was not alone and she was so alone
She wanted a horse
The horse of her dreams to ride on each day
To love and to cherish and take her away
To gallop into the clouds
Clouds of each season
The sky was an endless friend
For the sky was vast

There's a Space

It's between me and you
It's stabbingly silent,
It steals my words
Yet in my head is a longing to join you
And a fear of getting sucked in and losing me
There's a space between me and you
It's stabbingly silent, it steals my words
Yet in my head is a confusion
A raging anger a volcanic temper
That may fly off the wrong handle
There's a space between me and you
It's stabbingly silent and steals my words
I want to know how to join you
How to stay with you
And how to be true to myself
Yet I panic in fear of becoming absent
I fear you laughing at me
I fear my nakidity being visible
I fear your ridicule
I fear your jokes,
Your laughter and humour too
I do not get it's beyond me
There's a space between you and me
It's stabbingly silent and steals my words
My fear freezes up

Tells me I can't do it or be it
It tells me to leave, to run
It tells me I can't do social connections
There's a space that needs a bridge
There's a space that needs a voice
There's a space that I need to walk
There's a space that can become smaller
This space can have a boundary
Can I get closer than this lonely vacuum?
For it is empty here, so empty, so painfully empty
I see what I want and then move away
As if a fear of intimacy strangles me.

Can You See Her?

You may not know but she is here
You may not know but she is here
She learnt to hide
She learnt in silence
To hold silence as survival
It brought her here
To the hour the darkness became light
As dawn broke it created a time
It made a space where invisible becomes visible
There was a time you believed she needed nothing
There was a time you believed it was safer to be silent
For silence never let you down as it had no expectations
When silence broke and people laughed and spoke
Your anger rose and she slid away
They broke your friendship with silence
They intruded in your silent world
You felt unsafe and scared
You still do not trust laughter
You still do not go far with humour
Her best friend was Silence
Silence her biggest isolator
Silence was her biggest safety
Silence, she held her biggest feeling; loneliness
Her silence was her biggest friend
How you may ask,
How?

How confusing you say
No listen to the silence as it changes quality
Read the silences they have tones and rhythms

Does it echo? Does it warm? Does it freeze?
Listen… It's watching and waiting
For silence won over many years
It knew every smell, every move
Every sound and every site
And stored, stored in the silence
Stifled is this muffled voice
Shhhhh its OK
Dare she object "No, it's not
She hangs an invisible red flag for she smelt danger
Why do you ignore her?
Do you not trust her?
She did not feel safe
You bowled on IGNORING her
Shhhhhhhhhhhh DON'T Fucking, Shhhhh her

She said it was not OK
Shhhh Silence is the ruler, well it was
Silence means you manage
You know she gave up fighting it became pointless
She carried her head in silence and imprisoned any thoughts
She wrapped her voice in silence and had no audible opinion
The voice held shame
The voice was bad and always wrong
She promised, one day you will be free
Dream of being free from these walls
It seemed Death maybe the only freedom from these darkened walls
Did he die to be free?
Did she need to follow suit?

How long was silence a survivor
When will she be free from YOU?
You suffocate her
Anytime she tells you it is not OK
You just say Shhh you shroud her in Shhhh
Do not cradle her, she is not a baby
Do you think about her?
Fuck you… what about her – she is trapped
She is fed up with shhhh
She is fed up with being the good object,
The girl who helps and does to please,
It was important to be needed
You want her, yes, have no doubt she will accept
Yes, we… Yes, she will
(A royal we you understand)
Well, no more
She will learn to say No
Are you ready to break the code of silent obedience?

Cooeee do you see her
For she is not a baby,
She is a silenced adult
She is a silenced woman
She values silence
She values her senses
Then you devalue everything by accepting and singing Shhh,
And giving her the Shh effect as if a lullaby
She will find words
She will find voice
She will no longer hide in shame

Beyond Don't Know

When I see the red flag, I will speak
I may still say Don't know or yes when I mean no
I will try to hear my inside feelings
It's going to be a tough, tough ride
How can voicing the words of silence
Feel so hard and so strange
You may not know, I am here
I am learning to speak beyond "Don't know"
Learning to stand in the light of day
Stand in the Dawn, as the sun rises,
Rises at the beginning of the horizon
Lifts above the silent world creating a voice
A world with shared voice
Where silence is not the only tool
Where thrival is a cocktail of expression
To hold silence in honour
To hold voice in majesty
To be seen on the stage, the stage of your life
To stand with presence
Silence, it brought me here
To the hour the darkness became light
Just as dawn broke and the gold warmed through the frozen world
Icicles are flowing into the river of my soul
Dancing through my veins like the tenderness of life

The fragility has strength
Strength to trust my voice
Dance like the clouds
Like the clouds are dancing on the earth
Like the grass is singing in the sky
Whispering no more
Being in the breeze,
I feel my breath as if for the very first time
No longer holding my breath, I see my chest rise and fall
I feel warmth float from me, I feel my breath move
It is no longer frozen; I am becoming alive
Like I am standing on my head in the ocean
Breathing into my life
Living it my way with my head held high
With belonging in my adult self
Not hiding my buried child
Climbing into my own self
Who is this?
I wonder as I see you being you
Can I see me being me?
As I claim my voice and I claim all my cells
Can you see me?

Bathed in Silence

Bathed in silence
Gnawing at a hole
A whole pain
Bewildered and afraid as they paused
What would you make her do?
Her leg started a pendulic swing
Her heart started racing, pounding
She felt feelings inside as if for the first time
And you waited with her
The sadness came forth
A breath of sadness
Deep, wordless silence
And she was not alone
You breathed her sadness
You named the invisible tear
She stood bathed in held silence
It is a bath of black larva
Bubbling smouldering
Blanketing the sadness
She felt it deeply
The loss and her lost start
Where she had everything and
Was an emotional orphan bathed in silence;

She's standing on the island
She sees you all looking
She hears you all needing
She will help you
And she will help you
She'll help you too
She will do anything,
Anything you need
Oh yes
And you and you and you
And suddenly she is formed
She is formed by your request
She says yes to please
she bends any way to please
she cannot do it all and she tries
She cannot fail
And when the task is done
You turn away
She is all alone

Silence; Emotional Malignancy

Emotional malignancy bound in anger
Steaming below the surface
Stifled in a familiarity
The pattern of self-sacrifice
Accepting these inner wounds
In silence as each one cuts
And leaves no blood
Leaves no trace
It whitens the inside
It kills connections with life
The voice ruminates inside
It is at fault
If this were unleashed
She ploughed ahead on raging fireball
For she knew a volcanic eruption
Would leave years of unspoken devastation
She was afraid, to speak would betray
She sat on the turbulent wave of disloyalty
Containing, containing, pacifying,
For years she had felt duty bound and alone inside this ugliness
Fearing the consequences and shame
If anyone knew
If anyone knew, what would they do?
Run? Abandon ship? Seek cover?

And, and Then
Then she would be isolated once more in gut wrenching silence
Frozen out both externally and internally
Those bonds she had made she feared she'd lose
The time and journeys to connect were priceless
They were not all false or stifled
There are connections that are beginning flow
There are reservoirs and deserts to travel
The world inside is not joined, not yet
When the fragments collide, there is danger
How fluidity with one, created stalactites with another
And clings on like a stalagmite
Hence why she has been afraid of the thaw
It cannot come all at once for it will flood
Where real meets thawing it is scary and enlightening
Potentially treacherous as the crumbling cliff edge

A place where death meets life
A place where life meets death

Had She Ever Felt a Feeling?

She had never felt so sad,
She had never felt so lonely,
She had never felt these feelings,
She had never ever felt feelings,
She knew there words not their feel
For she had run, pedalled away endless miles alone
Away from fear
Away from sadness…
Herself and her silence,
Herself and her feelings,
Injury and ageing
Her body ground to a halt
Leaving nowhere to run,
And nowhere to hide,
Those feelings she ran from
Head on she now felt deep inside

Flickers of fear
Surges of heat
Panic as a ball of fire
Prickly fire
Rushes of rage
Frozen cold
Gripped in worry
Snuffled, blanketed in silence

Injury and ageing
As her body ground to a halt
With nowhere to run
And no place to hide
All she had left was herself
She felt too much to share
For she was locked into grief
The loss of her mobility
Left her with no key
Nowhere to run
No key
Nowhere to hide
And so, she began to find
A new route
To feel her lost feelings

Afraid of Her Dark

For years she sought light
Seeking a reason; a purpose
She loved her work and her connections
And then she felt empty
At times, there were moments
When the shadows got ever bigger
Ghosts of her roads
And then she was afraid of being left in her dark
And still is afraid of being left in her dark
The dark yanks a big sick feeling
Deep from the pit of her gut
One she did not feel before
As she ran many a mile for sure
She remembers darkness and how the light crept in
In hospital she would sit and wait
Would anyone know she was there alone
Would anyone come? Would anyone call?
For months terrified she watched
She watched the victims stream off to ECT
She wondered would that be her road?
It never was however,
Watching people gather she was absently wired
Looking for the rules
Escaping was the safest as fear overruled
There she was with no adult skill

She had been a child adult
Depersonalized to the core
Amongst a world she did not understand
As she wandered through the dungeons of grey matter
She had no words to say "Don't leave me in the dark"
Was it her fault she was there?
Don't leave her in her dark.

There she was stuck in hospital,
Like a goldfish in a bowl
Like a crab in a net
Like a cod on a line
Hooked through its palette
Or a dolphin in the arctic
Of a seal in the Sahara
Out of zone – zoned out
Trapped inside waiting alone
Waiting in the unknown
Don't leave her in her dark

Toothpaste

The last pearl of toothpaste
At the far end of the tube
No matter how hard you squeeze
It is stuck hibernating
Wishing to not be found
And its protection needed
To coat the tooth for life
It is shy
It stays away and wants out too

The last phase of natural life
So many are dying leaving their flocks
They are making rites of passage
She does not know how
How to find peace with her natal home
Or even if she can
She freezes there and has no audible words
Her words are padlocked inside a trunk of avoidance
She will not pass the gate
She holds the rules of silent compliance
Locked by a fear to upset
A fear to offend
Silence is not golden
For her it is agonizingly sore
She wants to know their wishes
And knows the gate of no go
Shall not be touched

Sentenced

Her life sentence began at her first breath
When she needed to be held and she probably was
And she was left to cry…
Was this her mother's tears?
With the hidden pain the secret miscarried child?

Seeking for soul dignity emotions were switched off
Turn off the tears, the rage and any sense of hope
Safety survival in a doer suit and please everyone

And now she finds soul dignity needs to come from within
Within is a tangle of disappointment
Sadness, loss and mystery around the unspoken shame
Whose is this silent ghost?
Compliantly silenced by loyalty and duty
Voiceless secrecy

She finds herself knotted in a dilemma
Like a tangled tight walk of life rope
She walked this walked trying to make it better for others
The reality is inside she is on her own
To exist she shelters her feelings and her thoughts
So, then she ponders, to exist or not to exist?
To be true and real or not real
To have a sense of belonging or freedom

Freedom - Escaping the feeling or owning the feelings

For survival she turned her back on known safe
The childhood sentence;
The routine; home school home
The prison of safety
Of being kept like a clockwork wax model;
of a daughter from the Victorian era
Cold generational gifts of frozen emotions
The utter starvation of authenticity
Filled with food that gave birth to the egg of silence
An impenetrable cocoon
The familial world that gave no integral love
Gave no contained holding
Gave a wish for others homes
To be another and not her

Word Paralysis

The girl, she watched her father's word paralysis
He stumbles in his stutter and slur
Silenced by a woman of power
Driven by fear
The girl, she must provide dutifully
Her dance to ease the void
She knows so well the woman's need
Her need for approval and control
The woman was in complete control for she was afraid of loss
The girl's fear's of the woman's deep depressive weep
Meant holding voice, obedience and respect

In silence, behind the scenes she watched the show
Vowing never to have a child and longing to, too
She was handcuffed to her mother
Tied by the apron strings that nobody could see
Once unlocked the rollercoaster of survival began
Dresses in a suit of addictive patterns
She had no chance to see the world that you lived in

For she was lost in the stillness
Running to feel alive as her hope evaporated
She was all at sea, lost in the atmosphere
Her emotionlessness lingered like a curtain bathed in cigars
Resulting asthma left her in breathless stress
As her inadequacy burnt

Her emptiness echoed in hollow time
Like the wooden belly of a grandfather clock
The pendulum clunks, back and forth
And stops until it is noticed but she was not
And the gear wound to find it's Tick Tock
All alone stood the heart-beat of the house
She listened to the minute's tick bye
The hours symbol clanged, another hour

Deeply Alone

Alone hurts deeper than any wound once inflicted by her hand
The quiet both relieves and disturbs
Awakens an inner doubt
A voice, a story of worthlessness, a secret world

When you are reading a novel, movement and noises interrupt,
When you are watching a movie, noise and movement interrupt,

When she is gone elsewhere noise interrupts,
Movement too stokes burning embers of anxiety
Panic wraps itself around the core
She will lose her place in her world

Like a python in for the kill who swallows whole
No breath, no bite
It has a fear of being connected
So, she sits trapped and frozen
Will her life thaw?
Would it be like death in an ice cream
Melt to nothingness and discarded
A formless sticky puddle they pass bye
Abandoned, rejected, sneered at

Becoming an onlooker of the world
A theatre in which you do not belong
Not on stage, nor in a seat
Passed bye and judged
People pass bye and judge
Passed bye and judged
That is her world
For she is sat alone
They give no time to think why
Why is she sat there alone, silent and still
Miles from here
An onlooker to the world
She has a paralysis of breath
She survives
Gulping in Jealousy, bathed in envy
What did she do wrong?
Why was she so bad?
Why could they not hold her?
Why could they not love her?
Why was she left to cry alone?
Was it her fault?

Shame

It was clearly her fault,
It always had been
So, she felt
It was clearly her bad
She always had felt so bad
Horrible and alone

She did not dare utter
She sheltered from sight
She was longing and afraid to long
And afraid so afraid she forgot she was real
She danced into a don't know world
Avoiding the pain of self-abandonment
Gulped away, disconnected she made her own world
She daydreamed in a world no one knew of
Hence no one could interrupt
Survival perceives there is no space for her
It keeps her busy
For had she paused
And should she have been able to feel a feeling
She would have been speared with sadness and anger
It would have been a total wipe out
Drained the survivor out of her lifeless body
And left it rigid, white and wrong

The Inner Voice

The voice who spoke in the depth of night was a friend of darkness
The voice who was silent in the light of day was a friend of loneliness
The voice who spoke beneath the cells of the atmosphere was a companion
Who was too afraid to say No or to disagree?
The voice who knew peace was by compliance
The voice who knew to study and sleep
The voice who was trained to not be seen
It trained her body to slide with stealth through the house
Not seen, not heard, not existing and yet living
In the cellars of the soul not even a whisper to say what about me?
Silently and hushed she watched, she waited and she watched
Silent obedience the best route through life
It was this voice that starved her body and mind
Nobody noticed or spoke until it was too late
They said to eat then they were stuck
Disobediently she did not eat, this she could do
She spread crumbs too
Her action was her voice, it said No!
She felt she had had enough so she may as well disappear
As her bones showed more and more,

She felt she was winning hoping to gain friends
And yet she was losing and had no chance
She promised to be an honourable daughter and to eat
Could they really not hear or see the impossible promise
The empty soul that had never spoken
The soul that was never seen or heard
The voice that ravaged inside and smiled outside
The Victorian rules where children are not seen or heard
She had no words to speak while trying to fix
Terrified of your torrential tears; all unspoken
Were you depressed and afraid of losing control?
She feared the look, your anger, your fury
As it is was the gatekeeper of words
The fear of soap to wash her mouth if wrong words were said
A method she then used when she broke her anorectic fast
It made her sick just as the fear of being told off
It was not safe to speak, silence was best
There was a horrid grating inside it was safe from view
Silence gave a felt safety as it buried rage
It housed a deadened sadness
feeling-less-ness which was feeling full
The voice who spoke in the corners of the night
The darkest corners out of the loop of silence
Both at school and at home
She did not know how to join in
She heard then laugh and have fun
She was being laughed at, they were laughing at her
So, her deafeningly loud loop of silence was safest
Did you know you could be deafened by silence?

To Say Or Not

Shame or pride
To choose the less wise
She goes along with your plan
She has thoughts
She believes these will be wrong
So, she stays quiet
As if she is stuck in a motorway crash
What stops her saying what she needs?

She learnt to be alone
Then there was nothing to say
While being alone,
Alone-ness offered a comforting familiarity
A challenge-less destruction
With no objection
NO reading someone else's mind
And where does it lead?
It takes her to bog standard inadequacy
Lonely is pacified by helping
Like buttercream in a cake
Sweet and sickly bad

And so, she learnt to sell her soul
Anything to be part, to belong
Part of something she never knew

Giving away companionship to her soul
Giving anything, literally anything
If only she had been able to say No and keep freedom

She was searching connection
She was dreaming of belonging
And she was desiring an escape
Where does freedom be still and not frozen?

Inner Wheels

The inner wheels turn
The jewellery box platform spins
It spins to the rhythm
Outside the shared reality
The crisis stumbles and roars,
A raw cruel dance inside her mental health churn
A dance of intense isolation
Where loneliness echoes,
An emptiness calls melancholically
Words thunder inside with tornado vigour and speed,
A viscous demeanour

Did you know every time you draw closer to your family
She recoils into invisibility
On the day her guard was down;
She growled in venomous rebound
For she was hurting with no excuse
She feels inadequate

She waits for the critique to poke out
Then pauses,
She worries she is in the way
She is the outsider, outside to your family
She fears you do not really love her
Maybe you are better at home and she is better alone

To control her poisonous envy for what she never had
This would save the piercing look of strangulation
She gives as childhood pain bites back
She stoops in shame

She hates the way she bites
All over an innocent vanilla butterfly cake
And every cup of tea made for you
She feels so ignored just as before
As if she did not exist
As the choir of ghostly spirts sign
Like a vacant lullaby
No recognition of her existence
Or of their relationship
And so as her ghosts deeply haunt her
She feels like an intruder in your home

A Christmas Day

Christmas day the rain plunged from cloud laden skies
The day black as death in her broken body
Eerily empty mist lingered over head hazing the day
She could not run out,

Out the bleakness of this mildy set winter's day
It was a wet day of inner strangulation
Her body rigidised even more,
Every move ached,
She was broken
Those stationary sedentary days kill her
Like mains charged electric shocks
Reminding her of her need for stillness to heal
The need to move to stay moveable
A paradox of broken life
She wants to stay able

She sits with beautiful folks in their later years
Her inner vision of years to come
How can she sit and enjoy?
How can she be content and love others?
How can she be in their presence and soul happy?
When she cannot run?

She has a long way to go to find this place

She's in a mind body jumble
It hurts with antagonistic twangs
As guitar chords that harmonise and clash
Her heart loves and yearns
She will never freely walk

Her pain is too high
Her tolerance too low
She takes herself to another place
She just gets up gets out and goes
In going she finds inner stability
In staying in she grieves
Mostly an unspoken grief
Where dreams are left unmet

Another Christmas Wall

She was dancing, dancing on her floor
Nobody saw the dance
Christmas came, that COVID Christmas
It stopped busy; the busy bus stopped
She hit a wall, her wall inside
She was locked inside
Chained to a gate
Cuffed to a cage
A cage of emptiness
She hit a wall, her wall
Her vat refilled with emptiness and despair
She felt lonely again
Captured in the dark was the cage
Cold hard and metallic
She was locked in
A tear fell, it froze
For she was trapped in a cage, freezing
Blind in a chasm
Of her still body and static soul
It bit her skin,
It burnt her nakidity
Her shield was broken
She felt exposed
Her clothes laddered, tattered and torn
Fragilely vulnerable she sat on the covid Christmas wall

Covid stopped the world
She felt empty, alone and deeply directionless
Stripped of her strategies to help, work and run
She was stopped
Her body inside stooped in shame
Nobody knew apart from you
You held still as she wandered through her bleakness
You saw a tear and caught her eye
She felt trapped and you gave her a hope
She was afraid of losing herself all over again
She needed safety, to feel real safely
For it felt there was not even a bat in the depth of the dark
To wrap its wings around her and cloak the pain
The pain that was draining all blood and all life
The stench of loneliness lingers
Hovers when the world stopped
Stopped for covid Christmas
Christmas stopping felt
Felt powerless
Felt helpless
Felt hopeless
When will the world re-start and how?
When will her world start and how?

No Words to Say

Watched and Watchful

As she sits at a table
The family share a meal
They share stories of back then
The reminisce
She has no stories to tell
No tales to share
She sits and watches
She sits and waits
Family meals
Silently watching
Questions are punched
With Food particles flying
She dreads feeding time,
She has memories of feeding time,
Feeding time like a human zoo
She will not eat and be seen
Perfection was "nil by mouth" her ultimate control
It was all she had left
In hospital she was watched
She felt stripped full view
High dependence in full view
So desperately wanting to be seen
Where every move watched,

With stealth and stillness; her aim to be unseen
Just like in childhood she became frozen and invisible
Are they still looking? No
They are making notes and chatting and laughing
Laughing at her?
And she is still watching the watchers
Without any eye contact she knows
She is desperate and scared
For she is a citizen of nowhere land
With nowhere to call home

Pass the Parcel

Children shriek in delight
To her it makes no difference
She hears their squeals of disappointment
And she is silent
The music starts
Her heart races as the room opens
We hold the layers she is hiding behind layers
The paper with words
The shiny paper, reflecting, deflecting
The torn paper being shredded mechanically
Layers of life, life that lost form

The outside layer
You peel the edges of protection
What is inside? What will we find? We never know?
She brings an essence of loneliness
Sprinkled through each bundle
Years of individual wrapping
Now she sits covered in discarded wrapping
Underneath an unidentified static object
Each layer carries messages, she cannot name
Laced with threats in magic ink
You can see only as you brush with water
And wait for the appearance
Covering over the writing tarnished by years

Faded in time
Degraded is the wrapping of time gone bye
Parchment tied in frayed ribbon
Some gummed up, some masked with tape
What will be surprises on the way?
Slowly layers unravel as we meander
Her atlas, a map of time

She wishes to understand the layers of her parcel
That make her understand the constellations of pain
The realise the sequential consequences
As memories draw pictures
With written words as yet unseen
Scribing the past
Finding the present with hope
Experiencing feelings for real
Seeking their foundations to build peace and connection
As we meet, we peel back layers
As the music plays again; she freezes as she cannot hear
And she shrugs away.
We move on,
You come back
And she is gone
She is gone

Under-Void

She called it the void
And yet you found noise in the void
The drama that sits under this noise
Like a baby stuffed gagged
Bound in a coffin
A coffin with a view to the world
Single degrading glass pane that is fragile
Sits ajar to beyond
Yet she cannot get out yet
You cannot get in yet
She sees enough to see and not be seen
Enough to hear rumbles and not be heard
And of course, the critical intonations
But blocked from hearing warmth
Or believing warmth is real
Too sad to feel warmth
In a sea of sadness
For in being always empty you cannot miss warmth
There is no let down in loneliness
No anger, no energy just a rigidity
You are lifeless and stuck in the cold
Stuck in a coffin of life
This is her void
If she lets herself go there
She does not know the path out,

She stays in its eery quietness
Where it is not angry
It is quiet and even breath is hushed
It is as if the path of the bereft
Maybe the childhood hope was lost
She does not know where
She does not know when
She was not permitted to ask
The silence is grief
Wordless grief
Whose is it?
It is loud
It is both big and small
It is the hidden shhhhame

Hold Her

Just hold her
She longs to be held
Arms wrapped around and nurtured
Like a little person
She craves and repels touch
She just wants to be held

She is low sitting under a tear laden cloud
Trying to blow its density away
It won't go
She cannot see the rainbow
She cannot feel the sun
nor the rain
She looks out
but she is not inside
You look into her dark blankness
It is not you,
you have done nothing
It is not her,
for she has gone

She doesn't know when she left
She does not feel warmth
She does not feel your love
Yet she knows it is there

She knows she has love for you
but not for her me

She does not want to contaminate you
Her black cloud won't budge,
It blankets her
Renders her absent and uninterested
It lets her me float away somewhere
Somewhere nobody can enter
She seems blank
Blank, still the cloud hangs
it saves her from the unknown
Like a shelter from UV light

Silent Sobs

She cries to herself,
I want you
I want someone to hold me
I want you to hold me still and to let me cry
Do not ask me why, I do not know

I hurt inside AND it's not you
I grieve for unknown emotions
I grieve for my friendless childhood
I grieve for my childlessness
I grieve for my years of aloneness
I grieve for lack of happiness
I feel toxic and crave a playful childhood
I crave for what I don't allow me

And as she ran and as she pedalled
Mountains of miles
Endless searching
The question came of why?
Why do I run and cycle so far and so much?

I want to feel you, to feel your warmth
I want to feel your arms around me
I want to feel your love inside out
I want to smile; smile from my inside

I want to find my inside smile
I want to be still

She pondered could she be both still and full
She didn't wish to chase her I anymore
Can I sit;
Sit on the hill
And see
And feel
What is around me
Where I am
Find who I am
Can I feel touchable?
Can I learn to like me?
Can I learn to love me?
So, I can stay and really love you

Night Reach

She does not ask for you to hold her
She needs to feel your warmth
She leaves her sofa and the nest she made
She wanders to the cupboard
To reach in or not to is the question
She does not want to eat she wants to be held
Will a bite warm inside
It so won't touch the need
It may pacify for sleep
She does not ask
Can She pass the temptress?
Can She reach a thin-ether that needs nothing?
Can She ask for a hug before she sleeps?
Or can she pass by the feeling deeply seated inside?
Like an un-held baby
The baby who needed to be held
Who did not cry;
Who did not indicate she needed;
As she smiled and she was left
And yet her smile said I need you
Hold me just once but as she smiled,
She masked any rawness
She was seen to be happy
And there she was alone

And still, she lies
She lies willing sleep to come
Her mind is awake
She does not rest
Wrapped in the duvet
Blanketed in clothes
There is a divide his side and hers
How she longs for him to hold her
And dreads this too
And still, she lies almost breathless
Listening to him breathe
She hears him stir
She hears pain
It's starting to get light
And so, she rises leaving him to sleep
Wishing he would hold her once more
Then she knows
She does not want to be seen or held
And she scurries away to nowhere in particular
She fleas

Stormy Night

The moon lights the stormy night
The clock tick's bye one small second at a time
I toss and turn, no rest or sleep;
Something is going on
Something is wordless
Formless it leaves a bereft hollow
A big empty world
To shrink and starve
To feed and enlarge
It will not rest
It will not sleep
It stirs, it stirs my mind
Quickens my thoughts
Swimming in syrup with bricks around my neck
It steals my breath
What is it?

The baby cried
Warmly wrapped within and tied to me
Its surely screaming
Let me grow
Let my feelings go
I'll kick as hard as I dare
Beating with my fists
I'll tug and twist my wrists
Soon you'll hear me
And then you may be able to set me free
What's out there?
That you work to hide
I know you care
But I must confide
I'm longing to explore
Beyond the warmth I'm hidden in
The warmth that feels so cold
Like a cell of life
There must be a door
A door beyond
A door to living

Leaving Home

Sadness at leaving home
Sadness at losing her mother therapist
The first place of emotional security and nurture,
She now has to leave
Looking in to the garden
She fears the abandonment
Being forgotten as in the deaths she'd met
Her fear rose to a panic
Would she seek comfort once again in food?
Would this pop up to handle stress bound in hate
and dreaming to be free to roam an open field
It is this place that holds memories of love
The first signpost she had reached
As a toddler she learnt to stand
To find her feet
Now she feared this loss
She holds a treasure a vivid memory
As if she is looking in the window with eyes of longing
With a hunger for this care and a hunger for life
This protection and nurture like losing the first home of her life
An emotional hospital with a guardian mother
How could she be saying good bye?
She remembers being abandoned in that starched room at university

Alone, she hoped it would be an exchange for life
She will never forget the impact of being alone and unprepared
Now she wants to hold onto her therapist forever
And she does inside, she sees her face and hears her words
This woman a guardian mother just as she has to say goodbye
She was given a rock, a foundation and such security
She is now terrified and sad of the ending
The transition, the separation
She wishes she could stay for ever
And hold this pricelessness
She is scared to say goodbye and she wants to be free
The journey to here has been tough
She was almost out and almost free
She had filled her backpack with connections
She was fed ready for the tours of life
Protected and breathing
And yet this felt like surgery
Snip, a knot tied with no anaesthetic
For she will be here and you'll be there
Self-fending, she can she knows she found a way to live
Through you she formed a shape
Now she feels alone worried about the walk ahead

Primal Separation

She has now lived some life
She now felt some emotions that had been buried
Soon she will have to feel all and all alone
To live all alone without protection
Without a scaffold it's all too much
Once she left this body of serenity
For as its natural birth
There was no way to crawl back inside
For warmth and security
As a baby that cannot return
Through cervix to womb
It is alive
It has to breathe all alone
No more a dependent emotional foetus
It is alone independent they call it
She never individuated before
It smiles for safety
It feeds and it breathes
It does not know what is enough
It does not know full or empty
It yearns for holding
For love and connection
The one that touched inside out
Every part was held in embryonic fluid
Until that day

She's scared she won't see you again
She wants to linger for one more glance
She worries that you will disappear
Another chord broken
This one feels it will break her life
And she cried this living loss
Just one more hug
She cried inside
No words came and thoughts spiralled fast
"Please don't make me say goodbye
I don't want to leave
I want to be held always"
As she left
She took away the words
They will always be inside her

Unwanted
Abandoned
Shoved to the side
Discarded
The pavement was clear
Lost
Nobody was there
Alone
Her shadow stood
Cold
Looking at the emptiness
Hollow
Open straps
Left
A blanket lay between
Empty
And not a sound
There never will be
A child to call her own
The time has passed
The sun held her shadow

And the isolated woman
a shadow
The upside down feeling
Turbulent
The baron image
Grief
The unspoken mirage
tears trapped

She had never had that feeling
The spontaneous inner kick
The first drawn breath
The pirouette of tears and smiles
She had never felt womanly
too afraid
She had never wrapped her arms tenderly around her own child
Or held the precious life next to her or felt her heart beat boom in time

Pushed Away

Pedalling tears away
The sadness was inside her
In her breath in every revolution
It was her
She had to dig deep
Dig deep or be alone
Alone waves a wand of freedom and depression
It is not safe
The temptress of space
The hopes and dreams
Are not a quintessential cottage from a romantic novel
Where roses line the wall of the apple scented garden
She has to go back there
To those places of loneliness
Where her messages grew
She was pedalling hard
Up those damned endless hills
To move from the feeling
Only you know what I mean
Seeking solace
Searching for a view
They cannot move
The complexities are woven in a deeply made cloth
It would break too many hearts
She will not break an ancient mother child bond
She knows it is precious
A precious gift she did not feel

The Gift of Therapy

It was at that moment
At that one moment
She knew

She knew she was alone
She knew she needed to climb her next step

And she needed someone there

The Difference

As you will have seen there were a few pivotal moments where she felt a physical and emotional bomb alert to make her take a fresh look and explore again her inner world. She is thankful for her work and life that brought her back to become a client once more after more than 15 years. She had never thought she could find another therapist who would be there, like an emotional guardian. On meeting her therapist Ari, she knew she had this opportunity. This shows how she builds trust and learns about her unspoken voice

The difference now is she is ready to find words. Ari holds a new space virtual and so real. He is there still and open and asks her to pause and she can with the acceptance and connection

The difference
She has ground beneath her feet
She has foundations upon which to build
She does not have to hide
What has been hidden inside for years
He sees and holds
The pot holes she's diverted round
The craters she has fell down
And climbed out of blind
She has words to walk the untrodden path
She has feelings
She can feel
And he is accepting of my road
He asks her to pause and feel inside her wordless words
That is the difference
And so, the bomb alerts
Gave her a chance to explore again

Where are we going?
Are you there?
Is it OK to ask?
What do I do?
How do I ask?
My head is too busy
Fireworks lighting my horizon
Is it OK?
I just never checked
Can I ask for more?
And how do I end?

Do You Hear What She Hears?

For it is inaudible
Beyond a canine decibel

Do you hear what she hears?
There is not a whisper in the grass
Not a whisp in the sky
Stoically silent
Or has she gone mad
Like the branches in a hurricane
Discharging their yield

There's a sound
It's inaudible
That starts the tidal race
It has a scent
That makes everything scurry inside
Everything outside is stoically still
Still and silent and yet soooo loud

It's like a secret dance
To a silent tune
The dance is frozen with no form
It runs on vapour
It rides on currents
All invisible to the naked eye

Like meteorites it pops
Like cracking candy
At random it implodes
Sending fireworks through
Like shockwaves
And they see nothing
None does but you

As you come close,
Close to the edge
Of a barren landscape
from a banished world

As you stay still
As if you see the music
As if you hear the dance
Your eyes follow the invisible
The rhythm of paralysis slows

Endings Happen And Beginnings Begin

She waits for the words to stop,
The screen to still
To go black
Pausing on the emotional layers
And yet is alert
Looking, watching, waiting
Sad, the clock will run out
As Zoom closes
It shuts a hug-less door
She does not want to leave
She has a feeling
A feeling that comes too late
The time has ended
She thinks it maybe sadness
She has a sadness
To leave cuts this connection
The button just cuts out
The screen goes black

She is feeling this empty isolation,
In a way she has not felt before
As the screen closes
As we say goodbye
She feels a deep ache a pain
Because she knows you see her

As the clock prepared to run out for today
As she prepares to compose the day…
She cuts off in that final moment
ready to re-lay her layers
Maybe to push away the warmth
As a survival protection

On Feeling Felt

I've walked the walk
I've survived in many ways
I've kinda thrived
I've talked her journey
I've felt mad
I've hurried through over many years
I've worked hard
I've never had to pause before,
or been asked to pause
Wait, wait he says pause now,
I felt sad, he was right
I felt sad, very sad, deeply sad
Do you know how cold air stings?
Not a wasp sting, or a bee
A deep, deep sting
From the white cladden frosty morning
So now it seems time to feel the feelings
The unfelt feelings and that is sadness
It hurts, it had no pictures then
Fuzzy ones are appearing now
It has no words, not even muffled
It is sad, it is empty
Is love that empty?
Do you know how empty burns?
Burns like tasting toffee

As it turns on the back of a wooden spoon
Burns layers beneath your tender tongue
It needs filling comfort of a soft warm goo
Like freshly baked bread squished in a child's hand
And suckling to soothe at bed time
When it feels echoey empty
You maybe just out there
And I am here alone and empty
It is quiet and still
Why is sadness here?
Where did it come from?
How do I reconcile
How do I warm the frozen sting?
I feel alone in my frozen quiet Darkness
My mind fills the space I drift away
As I disappear from here are you there?
Can you help me stay here?
Here in the here and now?

A Beautiful Encounter

Little girl on the path
Is clutching her dandelion clock
Her hair is gently blowing in the wind
Nanny and Granddad next to her
The woman stopped to be
Be there, just there, just then
Celebrating this treasured moment
How many blows are there?
The little girl smiled
And blew and blew and blew
And then turned to the grass
And picked the woman
A golden buttery dandelion
She cupped her hands
"For you" she said
Her beady eyes smiling
The woman stopped
She lowered herself
To the child
"Thank you," said the woman
They smiled as their eyes met
Where shall I put it?
And she set it on her handle bars
Carrying this gift home
The gift of connection

With her own little girl
Who nobody had stopped to be with;
Or to celebrate an amazing discovery
such a simple joy
and a real smile

Your White Car

Driving down the hill; my bike hiking up
The sky is blue my soul awakens
You head towards the lake
She sits beside you, her head stooped
Her grey mane and wizened face
Covered by her straw hat she is asleep
Out of your rolled down window
You smile and say; "Nearly There"
As I ascend and you descend
Where? Nearly where?
How do you know where my there is?
How do I know where your there is?
Or where her there is?
A scene crosses my face
Imagine being locked in
Ruminations circling like a bird of prey
Unable to tell anyone and having to hide
Under your straw hat your eyes are closed
Are you waiting in silence?
Silence to stop your breath
This terrifies me
Insanity, imagine not being able to have a valve
Padlocked in a compression chamber
Just like it was alone, she is on her own
Being done to, being talked at with no dignity

And he believes she wants to go down
He takes her there remembering the love, they once had

Down to the blue lake
where the boats dance on the glass like surface
for there is no wind today
There she sits in her straw hat in his car
She may not want to go there
So why do they say nearly there?
Do you know where my there is?
The destination of peace
Is it the soul on the hill?
Is it the woman standing in the lake?
Ripples lapping at her feet
Like a silent dance floor
Wait…
Wait for the answer…
You can see it in her eyes
You can hear it in her voice
Like a torch of shadows
A torch in the shadows
A torch giving light
A light in the shadows
Shadows in the dark

A key to nowhere
A key to somewhere
A watch that stopped
Just as time that stood still

Please wait sit with me

I am scared
Just be with me it means more than the world
That I am not alone in my shadows
That there is a light in my dark

My head is busy
the world of being done to
as we journey this path
through my grief
sit with me
stay with me
where ever I go
This is the road that has no sign
no destination
be there with me
be here with me
so, are we nearly there?

Are we at a place where I can be
stay with me
stay by my side
breath by breath
toe by toe
until I can find my own walk

They are together and I am apart
I look at the screen
I see a melancholic sadness
My face has tramlines of years unlived
Tired and aged beyond my years

Girl, you look so sad
So alone so outside
It is OK just to stop
Just to sit and cry

Loss

His emerald and sapphire plumage were fading
As he desperately pummelled her chest
His crimson tail warning cars away
He needed her to breathe
Frantically he trod faster and bounced
She did not stir
Her fawn and brown plumage lay
Just as the moment she was hit
Nobody had stopped
He had watched from the hedgerow in disbelief
His love dissolved in tears
He meandered alone back to the hedge
Reliving that fatal moment
When one of her prized orange feathers
Brushed passed him
Whispering to him to remember love never dies.

She thinks of her father, his eye
Her father's eye
Now as a faded like a bluebell
In a pastel phase as the end of spring
Always alert for the air raid siren
Waiting for safety
To find a helpless comrade
Lying wounded in a muddy trench

Limp and white as his father would have found
In the first war of the world as the spring faded
Her father, he never went to war, any war
His paralysis kept him at home
Watching, with disbelief in silence
His eye now faded, a jaded blue, like a worn cloth
Thin over many years wear protected by a spectacle
Glazed preservation from the raw elements
Cloaked behind this frame he cannot weep
His anxiety slurs as he sits waiting for time to pass
There will be a time he will slide into a sleep
And he will never have spoken his truth to her
Which is strangled in silent obedience
Is it that of a child of an alcoholic mother?
Waiting for the routine nocturnal storm
Is that a child of an older father who spend time at war?
Is it that of a child who watched the world from paralysis?
Watching his dreams fade away just one more time
And showing harmony on the surface?
She will never know for he will never speak

Getting Hold of Polarities

Haunted child captured in the absent adult
Absent adult spooked by the haunted child
Haunted adult baby-sitting an empty child
If the adult goes out the child frets
If the adult stays in the child feels trapped
The child, she observes the world around in silence
Stuffing feelings down
If the child goes out
She worries what she will miss
What she will return to
The anger roasts
Then swipes out the side
The adult won't let her talk
The adult scared of the child's anger
Scared of her own anger
The child looks at the adult
The frown lines that transverse her face
Like her grannies did
The worry that she sat below for years
She cannot bear the aged face she is hidden behind
The prison of sadness
The child, she remembers the haunted look
When she looked just once at her mother's eyes
The deep black hollow darkness that went on forever
And ever and ever with a cutting edge

She never looked again
It was eery and empty it spooked the child
Who haunts the adult who holds her;
She traps the adult they have an Avoid-dance
You see it don't you
Well, I sit aside,
I see these parts
I wonder how do I greet them
The adult is worried by the child's need
The child who looked for something attach to
She hoped everywhere to find a smile in an adult's eyes
She doubted this would ever happen and she searched
The adult says she is OK,
She knew she had to be when she was a child
Now she knows there is another dimension
She can feel not OK too and has to understand her haunted child

Unveiled

As masks come off
The world becomes less careful
As if it is over- and it's not
She keeps hers' on, others seem to stare
She is afraid of it, afraid of being unmasked
Her masks served her a grace
And now a barrier she does see
She may go to blank screen shows
To jobs and tasks
She sees people as intruders
She keeps a face that offers no connection
Serious, maybe unfriendly and a firm face
It serves to keep them away
She feels left out, that beautiful exclusion zone
She needed that when she had no conversation
Nothing to say that they would want to hear
She can deaf out people on many levels
She sees them as a threat and that was back then
Now she is stuck for she does not trust
She stays in the shadows behind her covid mask
Beneath that are masks upon masks
That put miles between her and them

She won't let herself in,
She is a shadow at their door
She is welcome and feels not
She has nothing to say
She has no connection with them
She does with him,
He does with them for he is theirs
She feels abandoned and rejected
She says it doesn't matter
She hides in her mask
She has to find a focus
Her bike, a walk, a job, she will do anything
Anything to avoid this empty loneliness
No matter what the weather does
Today the weeds
And then she is OK
She cannot sit up here and watch the drama
She loses the plot, she is distracted
Why did she learn to be so alone?
It is her self-isolation that is the problem
If those rules stayed, she'd be just fine
Interacting just with him
The rules kept the world out legitimately
And now there are no rules exponentially her fear rises
The safety abolished -changed threat level rises

The grave grief
Grief to Grave
grief too grave
I cannot hate you 'til you go
I cannot love you 'til it's safe
My hate keeps me away
It buries any sense of love
I grieve for what I never had
And never will
And never can
I worried I would catch it from you
So, I kept me locked away
Soon it will be too late
And yet I do not trust
Grief too Grave
Grief to Grave
The Grave Grief

Reflections

Onwards we go
She sat in a field
The sun streamed across her face
and she talked about those things
She never went to before
And there it was there she could talk
The sun held her
The bench beneath her
And the grass touching her feet
She spoke

She wandered on
Her journey took her there
And there on the cliff
In the here and now
On her feet
She looked and she saw
And she paused
And she drew
She drew with words
Painted pictures with words

The distance
The horizon
The present with ripples and rustling leaves
and the future over there, somewhere
And she felt held in time

And from a window on the hill
She peered through the branches of the tree

She looked outwards
She looked inwards
She cried a tear
She was so far away
So far, far away
She felt her loneliness
Loneliness that she had made
Through a window of the world
She did not trust before
Now it was time
Time to build connection and trust
With her small self
As the sun
Danced
Literally danced
On the ruffled skin of the world
The jewels
In turquiose and emerald
Filled the emptiness
With stillness

And then
She wandered and meandered
Through the sculpture of trees
When she stopped for a while
Sitting on a soft moss carpet
And she noticed roots
The bare roots
She felt the sunshine
And she felt alone

And she noticed the palette of life
The world of green
Tones and shades
And the peace

The land had slid
The cliff had melted
And she had formed her own form
Separate and close
Independent and attached
And there she stood for many to see
And she was vulnerable
And she was strong
And she stayed there and saw
Saw many weathers
And many faces
She stayed open
And engaged in their view
She was her
They were them